| DATE | | | |
|---|---|---|---|
| | | | |
| | | | |
| | | | |
| | | | |
| | | | |
| | | | |
| | | | |
| | | | |
| | | | |
| | | | |
| | | | |

*TWAYNE'S WORLD LEADERS SERIES*

EDITORS OF THIS VOLUME

Arthur W. Brown
*Baruch College, The City University
of New York*
and
Thomas S. Knight
*Adelphi University*

*C. Wright Mills*

TWLS 57

C. Wright Mills

# C. WRIGHT MILLS

By Howard Press

*C. W. Post College*

TWAYNE PUBLISHERS

A DIVISION OF G. K. HALL & CO., BOSTON

Copyright © 1978 by G. K. Hall & Co.
All Rights Reserved
*First Printing*

**Library of Congress Cataloging in Publication Data**

Press, Howard.
  C. Wright Mills.

(Twayne's world leaders series ; TWLS 57)
  Bibliography: p. 166 – 69
  Includes index.
  1.  Mills, Charles Wright.  2.  Sociologists
--United States--Biography.
HM22.U6M456   301'-092'4 [B]   77-16057
ISBN O-8057-7708-3

MANUFACTURED IN THE UNITED STATES OF AMERICA

To My Mother, Barbara Gordon Press,
and My Father, Harry Press

# Contents

# About the Author

Howard Press was born in New York City in 1937. In 1958 he received a B.A. from Columbia College where he was a student of Professor Mills. Columbia University awarded him the Ph.D. in Philosophy in 1966. He wrote his dissertation on "The Aesthetic Basis of Whitehead's Philosophy." He has taught at Columbia University and The University of New Hampshire; he is now Associate Professor of Philosophy at C. W. Post College of Long Island University. He has published widely in the fields of ethics, esthetics, and social philosophy in such journals as *The Journal of Philosophy*, *Ethics*, *The Philosophical Forum*, *Art and Artist*, *Telos*, and *Philosophy and Phenomenological Research*. His publications include: "Aesthetic Obligation," "Whitehead's Ethic of Feeling," "Marx, Freud, and the Pleasure Principle," "The Marxism and Anti-Marxism of Wilhelm Reich," "Marxism And Aesthetic Man," and "The Existential Basis of Marxism." He is presently completing a book on the philosophy and psychology of Karl Marx and has volumes on Plato and Franz Kafka in preparation. He makes his home in Manhattan.

# *Preface*

C. Wright Mills is a major intellectual figure, an "opposing figure," in a late phase of American liberalism. He has been called an intellectual hero; and since the style was the man, he may also be considered an existential hero. Against this personal and historical background, I propose to draw an intellectual portrait of Mills, showing him, above all, as a socially and intellectually engaged American in a crucial era of American history. In a sense Mills died at the close of this era (and thus, of course, at the beginning of the next); but at his death he was struggling, as he had always struggled, to develop a stance—personal, moral, intellectual—for the era to come, our own tumultuous times.

I would divide his career into four phases: (1) the social struggles of the 1930's, during which he came to maturity; (2) his work on American pragmatism and, concurrently, his researches into the European sociological tradition, especially the sociology of knowledge; (3) the explicit critique, in the 1940's and 1950's, of liberalism and liberal expectations, and as a closely related theme, the critique of "liberal" social science; (4) and finally, looking toward a future Mills did not live to see, the Marxist phase.

The creativity of a great thinker springs ultimately, as Bergson said, from a certain image that haunts his mind—a critical image, which is first of all characterized by "the power of negation." And indeed, the word "image" does in this sense often appear in Mills. I shall therefore try to articulate, in its many ramifications, Mills' image of social life and, in particular, its bearing on Establishment social science, of which Mills was so severe a critic. More generally, I shall examine the question, which for Mills was an agonizing personal question, of the role of "The Man of Knowledge" in society. Here, in Mills' drive to change people's minds, his notion of "the public," his stance as a Preacher, there is a fateful ambiguity.

I refer to Mills as a Radical in the Academy. So far as the Academy is concerned, this he surely was, in his own perception and that of his peers, although his radicalism, early and late, wavered, flagged, and was at all times deeply ambiguous and ambivalent. But this, perhaps, is simply to say that he was a man of his times—a man of the Left in difficult times and, as Mills often says, in deep trouble. As Richard Gillam writes, "Mills . . . never became part of the academic establishment; in the East, as in the West, he remained something of a marginal man, skirting the edges of academia, sometimes joining its inner ranks for a brief moment of solidarity, but never knowing the intense fraternity experienced by so many."[1]

Central to Mills' struggles, both personal and intellectual (for as we have noted, his intellectual style was at all times deeply personal), is the figure of Karl Marx, both as ally and adversary. For as Mills so often emphasizes, the classic tradition in sociology has for a hundred years been in continuous dialogue with Marx. This dialogue I have made a major theme of my study.

One of the major sources of what Mills called the "sociological imagination," has been, as Anthony Giddens emphasizes, socialism—as ideology, as social movement, and, now, posing a great challenge to social thought, Marxist and non-Marxist, as one form or another of living society. Another source of the sociological imagination, according to Robert A. Nisbet, is religion. Both Durkheim and Weber, the two towering figures in the camp of liberal sociology, were deeply concerned with religion, and their great socialist predecessor, Karl Marx, perhaps the greatest irreligionist in the history of thought, early wrote that the criticism of religion is the first premise of social thought. The question of religion—in essence the question, as Marx put it, of "consciousness" or "life" and, politically, of elitism or populism—has deep personal significance for Mills, a one-time altar boy, and is a pivot of his own sociological imagination. It is the great question dividing Marx and Weber, liberal sociology and radical sociology, and, as such, it defines Mills' dual, conflicted allegiance. As Nisbet writes, "The most powerful single doctrine in the sociological study of religion in Weber's Germany was that of Marx, for whom types of religion were but reflections of types of society. The greatness of Weber lies in his reversal of Marx, through empirical and logical demonstration that types of society may, equally, be shown to be reflections of types of religion."[2]

If the sociological tradition has been in continuous dialogue with Marx in the decade and a half since Mills' death, sociology has been in dialogue with Mills himself. This is true not only in the United States, but the world over, including the so-called Socialist world, with which Mills had fruitful personal contact in the late 1950's. In the United States, a spate of books on radical sociology has paid tribute to Mills' influence, and more conservative sociologists have found it necessary to defend themselves against charges of anti-Millsianism. It is my hope that this study may contribute to the many-sided dialogue among Marxists, Millsians, and other social thinkers.

I am indebted to many people, impossible to enumerate, and especially to my students, for intellectual dialogue and stimulation. I owe special thanks to Val and Barbara Dusek, who read the manuscript; to Barbara Fish, Jill Dannen, and Jacqueline Fuerst; and to Sol Roberts and Sidney Roberts for their help in difficult times. The unflagging intelligence, patience, and cooperation of Carol Philips, who typed the manuscript and offered editorial assistance, has been invaluable. I am indebted, finally, to Linda Pierce, who drew the manuscript to completion.

HOWARD PRESS

*C. W. Post College*

# Chronology

1916 Born August 28 in Waco, Texas, to Charles F. and Frances (Wright) Mills.

1930– Attends Dallas Technical High School, Dallas, Texas. Leaves
1934 Catholic Church.

1934 Enrolls in Texas Agricultural and Mechanical College. Has severe emotional crisis.

1935 Enrolls in University of Texas, Austin.

1938 Married in junior year, University of Texas.

1939 B.A. in philosophy, University of Texas.

1939 M.A. in philosophy and sociology, University of Texas. Thesis, "Reflection, Behavior, and Culture: An Essay in the Sociology of Knowledge."

1941 Ph.D. in Sociology and Anthropology, University of Wisconsin. Thesis, "A Sociological Account of Pragmatism."

1941– Associate Professor of Sociology, University of Maryland.
1945

1945 Works briefly as special business consultant for Smaller War Plants Corporation.

1945– Guggenheim Fellow.
1946

1945– Appointed by Robert K. Merton as Director of Labor
1948 Research, Division of Bureau of Applied Social Research, Columbia University.

1946– Associate Professor of Sociology, Columbia University.
1950

1947 Marries second wife.

1948 Publishes *The New Men of Power: America's Labor Leaders.*

1949 Visiting Professor, University of Chicago.

1950 Publishes *The Puerto Rican Journey: New York's Newest Migrants* (with Clarence Senior and Rose K. Goldsen).

1951 Publishes *White Collar: The American Middle Classes.*

1953    Visiting Professor, Brandeis University.
1953    Publishes *Character and Social Structure: The Psychology of Social Institutions* (with H. H. Gerth).
1954–   Lecturer at the William Alanson White Institute of
1956    Psychiatry.
1956–   Professor, University of Copenhagen.
1957
1956    Publishes *The Power Elite*.
1958    Publishes *The Causes of World War Three*.
1959    Marries Yaroslava Surmach.
1959    Publishes *The Sociological Imagination*.
1960    Visits the Soviet Union.
1960    Visits Cuba. Publishes *Listen Yankee! The Revolution in Cuba*.
1962    Publishes *The Marxists*.
1962    Dies, March 20, of heart attack, in Nyack, New York.

# CHAPTER 1

# *Beginnings*

E VEN as an anti-American, Charles Wright Mills was an all-American. It is against this background that we must understand him. He was born in Waco, Texas, in 1916, one year before President Wilson went to war to make the world safe for democracy (while the Bolsheviks were making their revolution in far-off Russia). He died, after forty-six hard-driving years, and after a decade and a half as a prestigious and embattled professor of Sociology at Columbia University, in Nyack, New York, beside the Hudson River. His growing up—a small-town, middle-class, Catholic, English-Irish, military-school boyhood—encompassed the Babbitry of the 1920's, the bitterness of the Depression, the hopes of the New Deal, the burgeoning radicalism of the 1930's, the Texas Dust Bowl, Southern evangelism, the class struggle and, as he was fond of saying, "one man, one rifle."

As a child, of a "rather feminine sensitivity"—even in his rugged maturity his face would sometimes betray a feminine softness and vulnerability—he experienced, writes Richard Gillam, in his unpublished Master's Essay, "a painful sense of isolation from his peers."[1] As a grown man, he was always a loner and a rebel. "I have never known what others call 'fraternity' with any group . . . neither academic nor political. With a few individuals, yes, but with groups, however small, no."[2]

In 1939, age twenty-three, he left Texas, and the University of Texas, where he received a B.A. and an M.A. in philosophy and sociology—a year as an engineering student at Texas A. & M. had turned out badly—and enrolled at the University of Wisconsin. There, "a tall young man of herculean build, who could jump his *salto mortale* with surprising grace, a good sportsman with ball and bat, a

13

dashing swimmer and boatsman,"[3] he acquired a Ph.D in sociology and anthropology. His dissertation, a study in the sociology of knowledge, was entitled "A Sociological Account of Pragmatism."

Three themes, three problems, three deep concerns—three "troubles," as Mills was often to say, in a very personal sense—inform his work at its inception: the importance of ideas, i.e., philosophy; the deceptiveness of ideas, as socially determined, i.e., ideology; and the hope-for, redemptive, unity of idea and action-pragmatism, perhaps, or as Mills later insists, "craftsmanship."

Or as we may put it dialectically: The Importance of Ideas, The Unimportance of Ideas, and . . . well, C. Wright Mills, the Professor on Motorcycle, agonized over that elusive synthesis all his life.

It was indeed philosophy, and a certain bad conscience about philosophy, that brought Mills to sociology; more personally— perhaps more existentially—it was his experience as a Catholic in a Baptist region where most other Catholics were "low-class" Mexicans. For there is, or, as Mills would insist, there should be, a sociology of sociology and of sociologists. The young Mills who took ideas seriously, and first of all, religious-philosophical ideas—to the end of his life Mills retained a strong respect for clergymen and was himself, as we have said, all his life a Preacher—reflected on the ideological differences in his milieu; thus became critical of ideas— and perhaps hostile to ideas (seeing how people were subjected to them). Thus he did his first professional work in the sociology of knowledge, simultaneously blowing up ideas and deflating them.

As Robert K. Merton writes, in an account of this *Wissensoziologie* especially applicable to Mills:

What these schemes of analysis have in common is the practice of discounting the face-value of statements, beliefs, and idea-systems by re-examining them within a new context which supplies the "real meaning." Statements ordinarily viewed in terms of their manifest content are debunked, whatever the intention of the analyst, by relating this content to attributes of the speaker or of the society in which he lives. The professional iconoclast, the trained debunker, the ideological analyst and their respective systems of thought thrive in a society where large groups of people have already become alienated from common values; where separate universes of discourse are linked with reciprocal distrust.[4]

Thus one can understand the many crosscurrents in the book on pragmatism. First of all (as we might expect in a young man schooled and deschooled in Catholicism) is the problem of belief and pragmatically, of belief and conduct—the problem of life-style. This personal problem continued to concern Mills greatly, and fatefully, he tried to resolve it on an individualistic basis. To the problem of belief and conduct, pragmatism itself seems to offer a solution: Peirce's "Fixation of Belief," James' "Will to Believe," Dewey's belief-fixing "Inquiry." But the solution is illusory, as Mills concluded; for pragmatism itself disappears in the solvent of sociology. That is to say, it is unmasked as ideology, justifying the life-ways, the political economy, in the broad sense, of various ascendant "publics." (More of this later.) Thus the book on pragmatism (surely, despite its rough-and-ready shape, one of the best we have) is an account of the place of pragmatism in Mills' own "psychic economy"—an account, as Mills frankly writes of James, of "what pragmatism does for [him], what function . . . it fill[s] in the economy of his mind";[5] and Mills' fond farewell to pragmatism—a farewell, to be sure, prolonged by many a backward glance.

But sociology is not only a solvent of belief, it is itself a belief. It is the belief in the primacy of society, normatively and factually. And this, in essence, is its place in Mills' life—what it "does for him." This is the dual, the dialectical, function of Mills' sociological imagination: to be at the same time critical and affirmative. This, both shy and stubborn, is the image that haunts Mills to the end, in the midst of the Weberian pessimism, the cynicism, the careerism. It is, in brief, the belief, the "Catholic" belief, which is yet, as pragmatism persuaded him, the scientific belief, that society really exists, that mind is social, and as Peirce wrote, that "the real is the idea in which the community finally settles down." Thus beyond pragmatism, or behind pragmatism, and the sociology of pragmatism, is sociology, the science of society. So let us for the present set aside the book on pragmatism, already a summation, and turn to the earlier articles on the sociology of knowledge.

In his earliest work on sociology Mills is already occupied with the two main themes of his life: belief and action. And when Mills gets down to work on these subjects it is, typically, as an outsider; a would-be believer, so to speak; a would-be actor. And perhaps, a would-be insider. (Robert K. Merton has written perceptively on the sociologist as insider and outsider.) Hence Mills' early interest in the sociology of knowledge, the topic of his first published paper. This European specialty—to which, as to other things European, Mills, the small-town Texan, was strongly attracted—originates in the

French school of Emile Durkheim (1858–1917) and was further developed in Germany (with backward glances, auspiciously for Mills, at Karl Marx) by Max Scheler (1874–1928) and Karl Mannheim (1893–1947). It is, as Mills understands it, a theory of "the social and economic factors operative in the reflective process,"[6] and a theory of "the social determination of mentality and ideas."[7] And this theory Mills finds wanting.

A thousand years ago, a thinker in Arab Spain, Averroes, wrote that there is one mind that thinks in all of us, one eternal, universal mind. As Latin Averroism, this doctrine was taken up in Christendom and ultimately condemned by the Church, as prejudicial to the faith, prejudicial to belief in personal immortality. A hundred years ago, in Catholic France, Emile Durkheim, the son of a rabbi, and heir to the collectivism of both Catholicism and Judaism, promulgated the doctrine of the *conscience collective*, the "group mind." (Despite his occasional disclaimers and numerous caveats by his commentators, there can be no doubt that this is indeed Durkheim's teaching.) Durkheim's corresponding deep interest in and sympathy for socialism, including Marxism, which we may infer from his works, but which antisocialist prejudice has tended to obscure, are documented by his student and collaborator, Marcel Mauss, in his preface to Durkheim's *Socialism*.[8]

Two generations later, in Protestant America, Charles Wright Mills, already a lonely figure, struggles toward a "thorough-going social theory of mind." Such a theory should not be a "traditional, individualistic theory." The individual is not the starting point for contemporary social psychology. And yet "ultimately reflection"— the testing of beliefs, as Mills writes—"has its seat in a minded organism."[9] And it is, as we shall see, ultimately from the point of view of the isolated thinker, the "minded organism," that Mills struggles.

Mills is on the horns of a dilemma. What he wants to affirm, and dares not affirm, is that the thought is not in the thinker (as later, with a somewhat different slant, he will argue that the motive is not in the doer). Thus, in his unpublished Master's Essay, 1939, echoing Mannheim (who takes, however, an equivocal stance on the question of the group mind), he can say, "strictly speaking, we should not say that the single individual thinks." But if the thought is not in the thinker, where is it? And if it is in the thinker, how did it get there, and how can it get out into other thinkers? And how, if at all, as Marx early wrote, does it "grip the masses"? "Rigor of beauty is the quest," wrote William Carlos Williams, another lonely American, in the American grain. "But how will you find beauty when it is locked in the mind past all remonstrance?" This, in a liberal time, is the question of the intellectual, and his public, of the philosopher, the man of knowledge, in society. "Where do correct ideas come from?" asks Mao Tse-tung. "Do they drop from the skies? No. Are they innate in the mind? No. They come from social practice, and from it alone. . . . It is man's social being that determines his thinking."[10]

Mao then begs the question: "Once the correct ideas characteristic of the advanced class are grasped by the masses, these ideas turn into a material force which changes society and changes the world."[11] Once again, where do correct ideas come from? But let us hear him out:

Among our comrades there are many who do not yet understand this theory of knowledge. When asked the source of their ideas, opinions, policies, methods, plans and conclusions, eloquent speeches and long articles, they consider the question strange and cannot answer it. Nor do they comprehend that matter can be transformed into consciousness and consciousness into matter, although such leaps are phenomena of every day life. It is therefore necessary to educate our comrades in the dialectical materialist theory of knowledge, so that they can orientate their thinking correctly, become good at investigations and study and at summing up experience, overcome difficulties, commit fewer mistakes, do their work better, and struggle hard so as to build China into a great and powerful socialist country and help the broad masses of the oppressed and exploited throughout the world in fulfillment of our great internationalist duty.[12]

An image of China is indeed deep in Mills' mind at this time, and in a sense, perhaps prophetically, at all times; for in 1940 he publishes an essay entitled "The Language and Ideas of Ancient China." The essay reviews the work of Marcel Granet, a Durkheimian Sinologist, and pays elaborate tribute to the French school of sociology, soon to be eclipsed in Mills' mind by the German school, especially Max Weber, who takes a much more jaundiced view of "social solidarity" than Durkheim. As befits a young scholar first trying his wings the essay is many things: sociology of language, sociology of knowledge, sociology of religion. But most of all, it is a deeply felt celebration of ancient China, and especially the Chinese mind. (As first presented in Howard Becker's seminar at Wisconsin, it was entitled "The Chinese Mentality as Analysed by Marcel Granet.")

The image of China and of Chinese mentality yielded by Granet's work is a profoundly conservative one; it is an image "traditional and sacred," and yet profoundly naturalistic, embedded in nature. "There is nothing in Chinese literature which corresponds to the 'spiritualism' of the West," declares Mills.[13] It is, above all, as Marxists are fond of saying, an image of the "totality," and a totality wrought in a certain magical sense which is always attractive to Mills, the would-be Preacher, by language:

This Sino-Tibetan language is shot through with emblems. It is heavy with judgments of value. It does not conduce to an impersonal and objective expression. Granet's analysis of the Chinese language discloses its controlling function to be an ideal of moral, social, and ritualistic *efficacy*. . . . The ideal of efficacy definitely outruns the philosophical mentality which would seek definite conceptions. It is not organized for the purpose of noting concepts, analysing ideas, or discursively exhibiting doctrines. It is fashioned entirely for the communication of sentimental attitudes, the suggestion of lines of conduct; to convince and convert.[14]

Mills, at age twenty-four, a one-time altar boy, clearly finds Granet's image of China profoundly liberating, as we see in the following panegyric: (Not until the Cuban experience, twenty grim, gritty years later, will he permit himself such a luxury.)

Even today, missionaries in distant areas of China admit that they are not able to teach the doctrine of the Fall or of Original Sin. Man owes all to civilization and civilization owes to man harmonious equilibrium, a sanctity, the quality of his being. The Chinese never consider man as isolated from his society. And society is never thought of as isolated from nature. They do not dream of placing underneath them some vulgar reality, nor above them a world of purely spiritual essences. Nature forms a single realm. A unique order presides over a universal life. And it is this order which imprints itself upon civilization. . . . There is no God, there is no law. . . . Tao is the supreme category; and that is why the chiefs must be sacred and learned. All Authority rests on reason.[15]

Thus, the Chinese mind is everything the Western (American?) mind is not: synthetic rather than analytic; holistic rather than piecemeal; value-laden rather than value-neutral; in a word nonscientific. Above all, the Chinese mind is integrative. It integrates nature, society and mind, thought and action, value and fact, the written and the spoken, male and female, old and young, rich and poor, strong and weak, rulers and ruled. It integrates, most of all, the individual and the collective, the one and the many. And this, indeed, is the deepest dream of sociology and of Mills' own sociological imagination, although he comes, in the Weberian fog, to perceive this only dimly.

It is one of Mills' purposes, in this essay on the Chinese mentality, "to trace the mechanisms connective of mentality and society."[16] Here, as so often in Mills—so often indeed, in the history of thought—we are at a crossroads, the crossroads of spiritualism and materialism. (Mills explicitly disavows spiritualism, but it is mentality that is his first consideration). These crossroads may be seen as Marx wrote, as the juncture of the German ideology, "which descends from heaven to earth," and the true "science of history," nascent Marxism, which "ascends from earth to heaven":

In other words, to arrive at man in the flesh, one does not set out from what men say, imagine, or conceive, nor from man as he is described, thought about, imagined, or conceived. Rather one sets out from real, active men and their actual life-process and demonstrates the development of ideological reflexes and echoes of that process. The phantoms formed in the human brain, too, are necessary sublimations of man's material life-process which is empirically verifiable and connected with material premises. Morality, religion, metaphysics, and all the rest of ideology and their corresponding forms of consciousness no longer seem to be independent. They have no history or development. Rather, men who develop their material production and their material relationships alter their thinking and the products of their thinking along with their real existence. Consciousness does not determine life, but life determines consciousness. In the first view the starting point is consciousness taken as a living individual; in the second it is the real living individuals themselves as they exist in real life, and consciousness is considered only as their consciousness.[17]

Mills, in this early essay, as ever after—a perpetual "religious crisis," in a sense—is divided at the crossroads and attempts to go in both ways, or perhaps in neither way. Thus he writes, "What is central and essential [in Granet's book] is the detailed marking of the 'parallelism' between ideas and societal features. He does not appeal to a generalized 'spirit of the times,' or some such ghost, but attempts to explain ideas in terms of the concrete history of a social system."[18]

But the "ghost," the premise of spiritualism—the religious premise, Weber's "spirit [*geist*, i.e., ghost] of capitalism"—dies hard, and it often seems, in this early essay by Mills, as befits the Weberian he is soon to become, and fatefully for the Marxist he has been and is later to become, that mind is the substratum of society, and not society that of mind. For whereas Marx writes that life—

biological and social—determines consciousness, it was Weber who "refuted" Marx with his book on *The Protestant Ethic*, a study of how a system of life is underlaid by consciousness, by religious belief; how an economic system is created and supported by a system of ideas.

The matter, of course, cannot be proved—indeed, the present volume assumes a certain religious or ideal "causality," and Weber himself writes that it is not his aim "to substitute for a one-sided materialistic an equally one-sided spiritualistic causal interpretation of culture and of history"[19] but must be judged broadly, heuristically, in accordance with broad principles of world view. But it must be remarked how strange it is, from Marx's point of view, to argue, as Weber does, that "the spirit of capitalism . . . was present before the capitalist order";[20] that a presumably self-originating ghost somehow brings a whole world into being. (And thus Weber himself writes that the capitalist ethos "had to originate somewhere, and not in isolated individuals alone, but as a way of life common to whole groups of men. This origin is what really needs explanation.")[21]

The question of "the balance between 'ideal' and 'material' factors in historical change" has been treated by Talcott Parsons, Weber's translator. (Broadly, it is also the question, so crucial to Mills, of "motivation"—motive power, personal and historical.) That it is not without existential import is indicated by the fate of Mills' image of China under Weberian influence. For the line of development Weber traces, in his inversion of Marx, leads "spiritually," as we shall later see more clearly, to the "Iron Cage" and the "No Exit" of capitalist hegemony; or, as, Mills will come so often to say, to the "Cheerful Robot."

With a slight shift of emphasis, the image of society which so powerfully attracts Mills—the profoundly humanistic, naturalistic Way (Tao) of ancient China—becomes a fallen image, and Mills loses his Way. The confidence in society, as a sphere of self-realization, the "vision of human society as the ultimate good," as C. B. MacPherson writes, and of "the ultimate value of living together,"[22] fails; thus, society becomes a system of "social control," and the search for community becomes a flight from community.

Nowhere is this fall—which is no cataclysm, but as we have seen, a slight shift of emphasis—more evident than in the theory of language, of paramount importance to Mills, who wants to build a sociology of knowledge on the "socio-lingual theory of mind," to Mills, the

Preacher, who wants through language to change people's minds. It is in his first published paper, "Logic, Language, and Culture" (1939) that Mills elaborates the socio-lingual theory, first formulated by George Herbert Mead (1863–1931), which he thinks will put sociology on a firmer foundation and yield a "thorough-going social theory of mind." In this, socio-lingual theory is the driving wheel and often the broken-down engine, of Mills' life and work.

"I wish," writes Mills, "to advance two hypotheses":

The first is derived from the social statement of mind presented by G. H. Mead. It is his concept of the "generalized other" which, with certain modification and extension, we may employ to show how societal process enters as determinants into reflection. The generalized other is the internalized audience with which the thinker converses: a focalized and abstracted organization of attitudes of those implicated in the social field of behaviour and experience. . . . Thinking follows the pattern of conversation. . . .[23] When we converse with ourselves in thought, a generalized other as the carrier of a socially derived logical apparatus restricts and governs the direction of that thought. . . . The function of words is the mediation of social behaviour, and their meanings are dependent upon this social and behavioral function. . . .[24] Mind is the interplay of the organism with social situations mediated by symbols. . . . Back of a vocabulary lie sets of collective action. . . . We can view language functionally as a system of social control.[25]

It is evident that there is in this model of mind, the model of the thinker and his audience, little "solidarity," in Durkheim's sense, little "communion," little sense of being of one mind; in short, little communication. (Thus, in Marx, division of labor is "the separation of labor from its object and from itself as one mind.") Mills' thinker is a lonely, isolated thinker, even solipsistic; for the audience is "internalized," and the thinker is talking to himself. ("We converse with ourselves in thought.") Nor is there in Mills' conception any "collective force," "collective ferment," such as Durkheim describes:

When individual minds are not isolated, but enter into close relation with, and act upon, each other, from their synthesis arises a new kind of psychic life. . . . It is, in fact, at such moments of collective ferment that are born the great ideals upon which civilizations rest. . . . This is the explanation of the highly unusual attitude of a man speaking to a crowd, at least if he has succeeded in entering into communion with it . . . he feels within him an unusual plethora of forces which overflow and emanate from him. . . . Now this extraordinary growth in power is something very real; it derives from the very group which he addresses. . . . It is no longer merely an individual who speaks; it is a group incarnate and personified.[26]

There is nothing of this in Mills. Far from "inspiring" the thinker, as we say, or being inspired by him, as in Durkheim's oratorical example (itself a plausible model of mind), the audience *conditions* him. "The audience conditions the talker; the other conditions the thinker and the outcome of their interaction is a function of both interactants."[27] Indeed, as Mills writes in his Master's Essay, where he covers the same ground, ". . . the thinker is 'circumscribed' by his audience . . . by the circle of meanings in which it understandingly sits. The process of 'externalizing' his thought in language is thus, by virtue of the commonality essential to meaning, under the control of the audience."[28]

This is surely a narrow and illiberal account of socio-lingual behavior, or to put it more simply, speech. For speech, is creative. As Paul Goodman writes, "It is a practical event." "Speaking is one way of taking and making a world." "Speaking is an archetype of human plastic power."[29] This creativity of the word and its origin in the human soul, attested in all cultures and literatures (and strongly emphasized, for example, by Durkheim), quite elude Mills' purview—again, through a slight shift in emphasis.

Thus, the same phenomena that to Mills evince cold conditioning and control, restraint and governance, reveal to another theorist of the socio-lingual a beehive of activity: "Human society . . . depends upon constantly operative communication. Deprived of communication, society would cease to exist. Only apparently and externally is it a static sum of social institutions: actually and internally it is revivified and creatively affirmed from day to day by particular acts of communication performed by individuals."[30]

Thus, in Mills's socio-lingual model of mind, both what is linguistic and what is social seem to go by the board, and language is wrenched from its living, social context. (Marx writes, in a characteristic materialization, and hence relative deemphasis, of language: "Language is as old as consciousness. It *is* practical consciousness which exists also for other men and hence exists for me personally as well. Language, like consciousness, only arises from the need and necessity of relationships with other men."[31]

It is, perhaps, not to such types, suggested by Mills, as the scientific worker, the preacher, or the spokesman for special interests, that we should go for a model of mind, but to the artist, the artisan, the fabricator and form-giver—Mills' own "craftsman"; to Balzac, Mills' favorite sociologist, or to Joyce, in his classic socio-ling-ual *Portrait of the Artist:* "Welcome, O life. I go to encounter for the millionth time the reality of experience and to forge in the smithy of my soul the uncreated conscience of my race."

The most important function of language, of course, in Mills' socio-lingual theory, is social control. "We can view language functionally as a system of social control." And as Mills continues:

It is only by utilizing the symbols common to his group that a thinker can think and communicate. Language, socially built and maintained, embodies implicit exhortations and social evaluations. By acquiring the categories of a language, we acquire the structured "ways" of a group, and along with the language, the value-implicates of those "ways." Our behavior and percep-tion, our logic and thought, come within the control of a system of language. . . . Thinking is the selection and manipulation of available symbolic material. . . . In manipulating a set of socially given symbols, thought is itself manipulated.[32]

How far is this (not merely through a translation into sociologese, nor by a total reversal of meaning, but, as we have said, through a slight shift of emphasis) from Mills' celebration of language in China, where words are "emblems," and "as emblematic realities . . . command the phenomena of man and nature." For "the word is not a simple sign or a clear and distinct meaning but an emblem, a pivot of life around which swings sacred constraints and solemn inducements. Condensed in it are all the values and virtues of prayer, orders, joy and poetic themes."[33]

It is true, as in ancient China, that language tends to move within the sphere of conventional society, and society within the sphere of conventional language; and that those with a stake in the prevailing order try to enforce the conventions of both language and society. But even in quiescent times new forms, social and lingual, new modes of thought and modes of life are continually evolving and competing for influence. And when social life quickens—a possibility unexplained by Mills, which in the form of the New Left, took him quite by surprise in the early sixties—then is the time of demonstrations, public meetings, speeches, agitation, civil disobedience, etc. As a (non-Marxist) philosopher writes:

The nineteenth century saw the rise of a group which in a very striking way broke away from the accepted form of common speech. This group is called the Marxists. It broke with the current philosophical way of speaking, with the religious way of speaking, with everything that Marx referred to as the bourgeois ideology. The Marxist way of speaking was so radically new that for a long time it remained unintelligible to many. Marxism was a real break-away from the accepted common way of speaking.[34]

Indeed, the forms of a language are not, as Mills writes, things that one "utilizes," "selects," "manipulates," and so forth. Indeed, these terms, in which Mills develops his theory of mind, are themselves forms that immobilize language and mind, in the service of repressive social ends. Why does anyone speak or write except to bring something into being that did not exist before? (Speech is creative: hence censorship in all its forms, overt and otherwise.)

This sociological approach to "the human," this behavioristic approach from "the outside," as Mills writes, has the characteristic effect of dissolving any intrinsic center of the human, any *root*—for as Marx writes, "The root is man"—and leaving all behavior open for socialization. This is indeed the main thrust of Mills' Master's thesis, which is largely a critique of Dewey's "biologism," his "biologic-adjustment model of action,"[35] in favor of the "cultural viewpoint." Nevertheless, as we shall see, Dewey's model of action continued to influence Mills strongly.

It is indeed, paradoxically or otherwise, in the service (largely implicit) of radicalism that Mills elaborates his sociological critique of biologistic pragmatism: "We are sociologically self-conscious; we have lived with the Marxists and found them at times not disingenuous." But once again, a main virtue of sociologism is its usefulness in the theory and practice of social control. "Control of behavior is through the field of stimulation," declares Mills. "That field is cultural. Behavior's forms and directions are culturally constituted and channeled."[36]

A main virtue of "biologism," on the other hand, Marx's theory, early and late, of "the material life-process," is its resistance to social control. In this Marx is allied to the instinct theory of Freud. "Immediately, *man* is a *natural being*. As a living natural being he is, in one aspect, endowed with the *natural capacities* and *vital powers* of an *active* natural being. These capabilities exist in him as tendencies and capabilities, as *drives*."[37] This providential resistance of man, as a biosocial organism, to external manipulation and socialization is much stressed by Lionel Trilling in his essay on *Freud and the Crisis of Our Culture*.

Now Freud may be right or he may be wrong in the place he gives to biology in human fate, but I think we must stop to consider whether this emphasis on biology, whether correct or incorrect, is not so far from being a reactionary idea that it is actually a liberating idea. It proposes to us that culture is not all-powerful. It suggests that there is a residue of human quality beyond the reach of cultural control, and that this residue of human quality, elemental as it may be, serves to bring culture itself under criticism and keeps it from being absolute.[38]

And if we do recognize this, we can begin to see why we may think of Freud's emphasis on biology as being a liberating idea. It is a resistance to and modification of the cultural omnipotence. We reflect that somewhere in the child, somewhere in the adult, there is a hard, irreducible, stubborn core of biological urgency, and biological necessity, and biological reason, which culture cannot reach and which reserves the right, which sooner or later it will exercise, to judge the culture and resist and revise it.[39]

Thus Ernest Becker, in his comments on the problem of motivation in Mills, begs the question when he writes: "The organism is active by definition of organism."[40] For it is precisely the concept of the organism that is at stake. In the book *Character and Social Structure* (1953), written in collaboration with Hans Gerth, Mills does indeed deal with "the organism," "psychic structure," and "the person." Now, "If we drop the metaphysical accent on the biological and the psychic and treat the person as just as 'real' as, and in many ways more important than, the organism and the psychic structure, we are able to enlarge our conception of motivation." And having accomplished this salutary economy, our enlarged conception of motivation yields the following, he continues. "It is a problem of *steered conduct* rather than a problem of *motive power*."[41] In what sense then is "the person" real? For conceived biologistically or otherwise—but I am arguing that in the last analysis there must be a biology irreducible to sociology to supply the "motive power"—"To be a person is to be an autonomous source of action."[42] This biologistic perception is strongly emphasized by Thomas and Znaniecki, in their sociology of the "creative individual": "The factor making the individual perceive and define new situations is always his own, conscious or subconscious, desire for new experience. There is no external power capable of forcing him to work out a new definition. . . . Even the mere defense against an aggression disturbing a state of security would be impossible without a latent power making the individual face the new situation instead of running away."[43]

It is this internal source of action, deep in the human organism, this "motive power," that Mills labors to deny. Thus, in the remarkable essay of 1940, "Situated Actions and Vocabularies of Motive," and again, in *Character and Social Structure*, a decade and half later, Mills argues, in accordance with "Mead's program to approach behavior socially and from the outside,"[44] that motives are not subjective springs of action, originating inside the individual, but "words": "typical vocabularies having ascertainable functions in delimited societal situations. . . . Motives are imputed or avowed answers to the questions interrupting acts or programs. . . . Motives are words. . . . They do not denote any elements in individuals. They stand for anticipated situational consequences of questioned conduct."[45]

This is a rather strained and paradoxical thesis—indeed, to my mind, barely intelligible (although, to be sure, of a piece with a highly prevalent sociologistic, especially Parsonian, approach to motivation). It purports to be a theory of behavior, a theory of conduct, a theory of action. But action is not merely people talking ("motives are words"); and the control of action (if that is what one wants) is not simply controlling what people say about their actions, what they avow as their motives. Indeed, Mills is eventually led, in his theory of motives, to the following *reductio ad absurdum*:

Individualistic, sexual, hedonistic, and pecuniary vocabularies of motives are apparently now dominant in many sections of twentieth-century America. Under such an ethos, verbalization of alternative conduct in these terms is least likely to be challenged among dominant groups. . . . A medieval monk writes that he gave food to a poor but pretty woman because it was "for the glory of God and the eternal salvation of his soul." Why do we tend to question him and impute sexual motives? Because sex is an influential motive in our society and time.[46]

Now we may say that in revolutionary China, collectivistic, Puritanical, and nonpecuniary vocabularies of motive are dominant. But it cannot be impossible that we may hear collectivistic avowals of motive and observe individualistically motivated behavior. We may hear, somewhat differently, a good deal of Puritanism, or what sounds like Puritanism, and observe a good deal of Eros. We may even observe behavior whose apparent motivation cannot be described in any vocabulary of motives that we know (for example, new sublimations, which are possible only in a collectivistic society). Even in New York, we may discover that an actress who thought herself motivated by selfish ambition, may actually be motivated, in a less cynical vocabulary, but quite beyond any vocabulary, by love. (I owe this example to Ms. Marilynn Brodnick.)

The most interesting case of course is sex. And surely, if sex is an influential and widespread motive in our society and time—as if it were not influential and widespread in all societies and times, as the deepest bio-social need—this is not merely a matter of vocabulary. (So far does Mills go to deny "motive power" in the human organism, so far, as we shall see later, is he an Anti-Somatist!) Thus we find Mills attacking "psychoanalysis with its dogma of rationalization and its systematic motive-mongering."

It is apparent that these motives are those of an upper-class bourgeois patriarch group with strong sexual and individualistic orientation. When introspecting on the couches of Freud, patients used the only vocabulary of motives they knew; Freud got his hunch and guided further talk. [47]

If it is true that these were the motives of a selected population group, it is not because these motives were avowed. Quite the contrary, they were seldom if ever avowed. The avowed motives were those of love, self-sacrifice, and duty. Nor were these motives customarily imputed in the society in which Freud moved. It was Freud who imputed them, inventing a new vocabulary to do so (look at any psychoanalytic dictionary), and brought down the wrath of this bourgeois world on his head.

Why, in the face of so many difficulties, does Mills advance this theory? What does it do for him?

The agent is in trouble, as Mills will later like to say. He is in trouble with the "inside," the pressures, the "motive power," as we will remember, of his own inner needs, and with the "outside," the pressures of the punishing society, which attempts, as Mills writes, to "steer" him. The effect of Mills' theory, in simplest terms, is to neutralize both inside and outside and relieve the pressure; for there is no inside, it has been conjured away, and the outside is merely conventional. This is essentially the upshot of the Grand Theory of Mills' antagonist, Talcott Parsons, in his approach to social action. Further, indicative of a deep current in sociology, the question of the "inner pressure" is one of the grounds for Weber's distinction between Catholicism and Protestantism: "The Catholic confession of sin was, to repeat, by comparison a means of relieving the person from the tremendous internal pressure under which the sect member [Protestant] in his conduct was constantly held." [48]

But this theory of action, both liberal and illiberal, liberating and pacifying, in relieving one sort of anxiety, only creates another. For then the question is no longer, "Shall I sin, urged by powerful forces within, or shall I abstain, urged from powerful forces without?" but "What shall I do at all?" This is the question, emerging in the dismal 1950's, of David Reisman's "Lonely Crowd," of people neither "inner-directed" nor "outer-directed." And it is the question of Mills' own "White-Collar"—the question of false consciousness, of the emptiness and apathy of the middle classes after the authority of both the inside and the outside has collapsed. In a sense, and definitively, we may suspect, in the case of Mills, it is a religious question, a question of "works," the Catholic exteriority, or "faith," the Protestant interiority. As we shall see, Mills does indeed pose this question, the theory of action, in these terms; and it is, fatefully, a question that, in the absence and nullity of both inner and outer authority, is unresoluble.

Now there is, Mills' theory notwithstanding, a very important sociological sense in which motives are not in individuals. And since behaviorism, through which Mills, "from the outside," approaches his subject matter, is still essentially individual psychology, a theory of individual behavior, Mills never gets to explore this deeply. This is the theory of mass behavior or mass psychology, for example, Durkheim's theory of suicide as a phenomenon of collective consciousness, a motive dependent on the state of society as a whole. Thus there is a *rate* of suicide, of crime, of drug addition, etc., which allots to individuals their chances. As Durkheim writes, "At any given moment the moral constitution of society establishes the contingent of voluntary deaths. There is, therefore, for each people a collective force of a definite amount of energy, impelling men to self-destruction. . . . Each social group really has a collective inclination for the act, quite its own, and the source of all individual inclination, rather than their result."[49] Because of special considerations, Durkheim writes that collective tendencies are "exterior" to individuals; we would prefer to say that this collectivity is interior, immanent; or as Durkheim, in an uncharacteristic locution, says, it is "society living and acting within us."[50]

A similar theory of collective, sociohistorical motivation, is an important presupposition of Marx's historical materialism; for example, in the theory of capital accumulation, in which in a sense it is *society* that motivates saving and investment, and not through a central authority but a diffused ethos. Likewise, there may arise a revolutionary ethos. This is the problem, just out of Mills' grasp, which becomes so crucial in his latter grappling with history, historical agency, historical decision making; in short, the all-important theme, which came to define his life's work, of the power elite.

CHAPTER 2

# The Pragmatic Pivot

THE year 1943, the beginning of the end of the British-Russo-American struggle against the Nazi behemoth, marks the completion of Mills' doctoral work. He was then teaching at the University of Maryland; and already, according to his close friend, the Leftist writer Harvey Swados, "a weird melange of Theodore Roosevelt and Scott Fitzgerald, egomaniacal and brooding, hearty and homeless, driven by a demon of discontent and ambition, with faith only in the therapy of creative work, whether intellectual or physical."[1] From a more academic standpoint, the historian Kenneth Stamp, his colleague at Maryland, remembers him "pacing and posturing, lecturing to his friends, warning them against the temptations of this wicked world,"[2] "always the outsider, always the rebel, always the slightly paranoic believer in plots."[3]

Mills' dissertation, *Sociology and Pragmatism*, originally entitled "A Sociological Account of Pragmatism," was published posthumously in 1966. It is an ambitious undertaking, a confluence of many interests—social history, biography, philosophy, sociology—and a program, a promise (only fragmentarily fulfilled) for future work. "Our most generic problem," Mills writes, "consists in explaining the relations between one type of philosophy, pragmatism, and the American social structure, 'between' philosophy and society; operating as a crude but most tangible link are the educational institutions of higher learning."[4]

The initial impetus for this project comes from Thorstein Veblen (1857–1929), one of the great outsiders of American intellectual life, whose work, especially the epochal *The Higher Learning in America* (1918), Mills had encountered at Texas. Through Veblen, the

30

sociology of mind, which so preoccupied Mills, becomes a problem of the *institutionalization* of mind, indeed, of the institutional *basis* of mind. As Walter Benjamin (1892–1940) the German Marxist literary critic, with whose work Mills may have had some acquaintance, writes, it is a problem of the "writer as producer," as an individual with a definite "position in the process of production."[5]

Now it is clear that the "free scholar" has a place in the process of production different from that of the university man. ("Only artists and free scholars," Beethoven said, "carry their happiness in themselves.") And this, already a point of great sociological importance—and of great personal importance to Mills, a writer-professor—sets the stage for pragmatism. For, he says, "The more mature proliferation of pragmatism has gone on in universities at the hands of university men, but it was initiated by men outside of universities." Thus, if "The history of pragmatism, is, in part, a history of the academic profession in America,"[6] it is in important respects a history of the decline of pragmatism.

To be sure, there is a sociology of the free scholar no less than of the university man, a sociology exemplified in the Cambridge Metaphysical Club, where pragmatism was born in the 1870's, according to Mills' very detailed account. The mind of Charles Sanders Peirce provides the best example of the sociology of the university man. But the mind of the free scholar is perhaps less fettered and impure; for he is an entrepreneur, competing independently in the marketplace of ideas. This idea is never stated explicitly by Mills but lies deep in his mind and may be found at work in his career. The university man however, is a salaried employee, whose income depends on business interests as Veblen showed in "The Conduct of Universities by Business Men." Thus, although Mills is far from suggesting that pragmatism is the philosophy of American business, he is able to write, with a muckraker's zeal: "It was at Rockefeller's Chicago plant [the University of Chicago] that Mead and Dewey worked out the major elements of their brands of pragmatism."[7] And a little later: "The Chicago school of pragmatism was developed in the center of a major vehicle of (1) class ascent and (2) professionalization. Its first public was drawn from those on the make within these two patterns."[8]

Now how is Mills going to situate pragmatism sociologically and carry out his purpose, a "Sociological Account of Pragmatism"? Here Mills brings together, in no very systematic fashion, a number of

factors, all of which bear on the development most important for
pragmatism, the "secularization of American society" and the
consequent "secularization of learning in America." Among these
factors the most prominent, the most inclusive, is "the movement
from an agrarian to an industrial social structure," with resultant
changes in "occupational structure" or "career chances," making for
the introduction into higher education of more "utilitarian subjects."[9]

The crucial question of this "secularization," this radical shift,
decisive for pragmatism, from a period dominated by religion, "in the
embrace of Puritanism," as Mills writes, to our subsequent irreligion,
Mills is content to call "a growth of indifference to religion which
directed attention elsewhere." With these casual words he dismisses
the remarkable movement, inexplicable except from a Marxist standpoint, from a period in which atheists were rare to one in which
even—indeed, especially—the clergy are atheists. Or in a wordy,
but scarcely illuminating formulation:

> The mechanics and structures which *set* the institutional base on an
> intellectual milieu [sic] "go on behind the backs" of the individuals
> participating in them. Nor are such shifts necessarily due to anyone's
> intention. The secularization of the schools in the United States was not
> primarily due to any sudden or gradual turn against religion. It was due,
> negatively, to intersect conflict and positively, to those middle class chances
> for ascent that were manifested by qualitative changes in the occupational
> structure, and which directed interests to the side of the complex of religious
> conflicts and careers.[10]

Here, I think we sense a relationship to Mills' own
secularization—the secularization, rather mysterious, as such things
are, of a one-time altar boy—and to his deeply rooted inclination,
both theoretical and personal, to look at things in terms of "careers."
And here also the quarrel between Marx and Weber, between
consciousness and life, the quarrel which occupied Mills all this life,
representing, existentially, two "life options," in the Jamesian sense,
becomes audible, a rumbling in the depths.

For Mills' question, in the most immediate, existential sense, is
basically this: How do we believe? (More precisely, more pragmatistically, I think, than *What* do we believe?) And genetically,
sociologically, and sociopsychologically, how do we come to believe,
and how do we cease to believe? And how, after a transition, or more
traumatically, a fall, from belief to unbelief, how, if at all, do we come
to believe again? And most important of all, how, as Peirce writes, do

we "fix" belief, and pass from our "uneasy and dissatisfied" state of doubt, as Peirce puts it, into a "calm and satisfactory state where we do not wish to avoid or to change to a belief in anything else"?[11] And since belief, as Peirce believed, cannot be fixed individually, but only in a community of belief, the "unlimited community" of scientists, how, from the standpoint of an isolated thinker, like Peirce, like Mills, do we build such a community, and finally "settle down"? This is a problem which Mills, through many phases of belief and unbelief, never resolved. It is the problem he confronts in pragmatism, in the Metaphysical Club, in Peirce, James, and Dewey.

The Metaphysical Club, a "knot of young men," as Peirce wrote, meeting in Cambridge in the early 1870's, "sometimes in my study, sometimes in William James'," is Mills' laboratory for the study of pragmatism, just as it was the laboratory and testing ground for pragmatism itself, according to Peirce's account. Here, in this small circle of free scholars, members, as Mills writes, of a "free intelligentsia," pragmatism was born. Here, in this intersection of lives, and of professional lives, "careers," as Mills so often says, is a focal point of intense and poignant interest, to the one-time passionate pragmatist, who had early embraced the pragmatic idea as a style of life and an authority, a methodology, for belief.

The Metaphysical Club numbered seven, excluding Peirce and James, to whom Mills devotes separate chapters. They all engage Mills' lively sympathies, and embody, it seems, different and sometimes conflicting tendencies in his own mind. As he put it, "We want briefly to catch the pragmatic mood and style, insofar as it exists, in each of the members of the Metaphysical Club."

Francis Ellington Abbot (1836–1903) was the author of a book called *Scientific Theism*; Mills is apparently one of the few to have read it. ("The pages of the copies in the Library of Congress were uncut in 1941.") He was, Mills writes, a "religious and social humanist." Like Peirce, he championed science and logical realism against modern philosophy and nominalism; in the terms for which these logical ideas are "surrogates," as Mills says, he championed the species, the race, as against an individualism trapped in "the magic circle of Egoism": "He not only wants to believe humanistically; he wants to plant it deeply [sic], as part of the universe, and his strategy is to lean it against the verity of 'scientific method.' "[12]

Chauncey Wright (1830–1875) was "at the center of the first immediate audience of Peirce's pragmatism." Like Peirce, he "was born and lived in active scientific work," stressed in pragmatic style "sensuous verification" as the hallmark of science and strongly exhibited, as Mills writes, a "feel for the push of this manner of thinking." But unlike Peirce and Abbot, Chauncey Wright was a nominalist and an individualist, and accordingly, his " 'liberalism' is hesitant." For Mills, "the socio-political point that is significant in connection with Chauncey Wright's style of thinking . . . is the linkage of *logical nominalism* with *political individualism*. In Peirce and Abbot 'scientific method' involves logical realism and neither Abbot nor Peirce is 'individualistic' politically."[13] Like Peirce, Chauncey Wright relegated religion to the sphere of the practical.

John Fiske (1842–1901) became a well-known writer on philosophy and history but was without "a pragmatic component." Nicholas St. John Green (1830–1876), a lawyer, is cited by Peirce as "the grandfather of pragmatism," for "he often urged the importance of applying Bain's definition of belief, as 'that upon which a man is prepared to act.' " Of Oliver Wendell Holmes (1842–1935), the future Supreme Court Justice, Mills writes: "Of all the individuals who may be termed 'pragmatist' Holmes alone has recognized the use of force and power involved in 'pragmatism,' and only he accepted an institutional position of power."[14]

Here, in the Metaphysical Club, the idea of a public, so crucial for Mills, is exhibited concretely but not precisely in the terms of Mills' conscious usage. For here the thought is not in the isolated thinker—"C. S. Peirce thinking," arising inexplicably from "inside" or "outside," and addressed to a more or less remote and passive audience—but emerges, constitutes, and is constituted by a many-sided dialogue. And this dialogue is itself constituted, in the manner of Walter Benjamin's formulation, by the place in the "production process" of the dialogists; or as Mills writes, by the kinds of "professionals" taking part in it. As Mills, still reaching for a social theory of mind, sums it up:

These seven men constitute the first explicit public of what later became pragmatism. From all indications, it was against them and with them that C. S. Peirce was thinking during the writing of his statement [the statement of pragmatism, the pragmatist manifesto, quoted above]. . . . By grasping the lives of these men, their opinions and interests, their positions in the social structure of nineteenth century New England, we are enabled to catch the larger secular and professionalizing movement of intellectual affairs.[15]

Of Charles Sanders Peirce, the reclusive founder of pragmatism, Mills writes: "Two major facts may be taken as outstanding. . . . He was an active scientist and he was an outsider in philosophy."[16] Born "of purest Puritan stock," in 1839, the son of Benjamin Peirce, a prominent mathematician and scientist, Peirce came early to what Mills calls the "laboratory style of inquiry." In this he was very much his father's son, a theme of some importance to Mills: "From the beginning his father wanted him to be a scientist, setting up heavy expectations in this direction."[17] Graduating from Harvard in 1863, with a degree in chemistry, Peirce pursued a varied career, as a chemist, coastal surveyor, astronomer, and briefly, from time to time—for only eight years during his entire life, Mills emphasizes—a teacher of philosophy. He died in obscurity and hardship in 1914. "He was," says Mills, "a 'frustrated' and 'isolated' man: a writer without a publisher, a 'teacher' with scarcely a disciple, largely unknown to any public."[18]

"The central imputation" of Peirce's life, once again, is his character as a scientist and an outsider. An outsider he certainly was; but it is not altogether clear why pragmatism should be an outsider's philosophy, especially when it is also an insider's philosophy, the philosophy, as we have seen, of those "on the make" within the system. Also, I suspect that Mills rather overrates Peirce's scientific bent, and that Peirce's self-imputation in this regard, which Mills quotes extensively ("I was brought up in an atmosphere of scientific inquiry, and have all my life lived chiefly among scientific men"), should not be taken wholly at face value. For it is doubtful that problems of doubt and belief arise in scientific work in quite the same way they arise in Peirce's thought. Rather is this a pragmatist theory of science, a theory which arises in an essentially religious context, or in reaction against religion; against, as Mills himself notes, the Protestant interiority.

For science, as Peirce writes, is only one method of "fixing belief," although probably the most effective, the others being "the method of tenacity," "the method of authority," and "the method of taste." The method of tenacity, an individualistic method, consists simply in holding tenaciously to an opinion, whatever it may be; the method of authority, in letting "the will of the state act . . . instead of that of the individual"; the method of taste, more obscurely, in believing what seems reasonable to most people in your milieu.

The method of science is immediately advantageous because it determines our beliefs, "by nothing human, but by some external permanency—by something on which our thinking has no effect."[19] But this external permanency is itself, in rather Kantian fashion, determined by belief, by the unlimited community of scientists, stretching infinitely into the future; and the ultimate advantage of science, as a method of fixing belief, is that it is a communitarian principle to the fullest degree: "the seat of authority," as Mills writes, "is within the community of scientists."[20]

Based on this social principle, science enables us to escape from the narrow circle of egoism, of "immediate consciousness"; the Cartesian circle, as Mills writes, of individualistic doubt and individualistic belief. "The Cartesian concept of doubt is a component of a larger conception of methodology," says Mills.[21] "Against this conception of method, doubt, intention, and logic, Peirce, in the 1880's, presented a set of demands, instituted a positive critique."[22]

The existential import of Peirce's pragmatism, which is very clear, as we shall see, in the pragmatism of William James, is that from this sphere of "Protestant epistemology,"[23] as Mills writes, this "Protestant appeal to immediate consciousness,"[24] this Puritanical consciousness, we may break out into the sphere of works. From this Cartesian-Protestant sphere of faith, hope and despair, the sphere, as Marx writes, of the "abstract thinker," a "pure, restless, revolving within itself,"[25] we may break out into action, pragmatic action, the practical—or, as Marx wrote, praxis.

But here Peirce proves disappointing. For "These conceptions are thoroughly insulated from the sphere of 'practice,' "[26] and Peirce's pragmatism is "anti-practicalism."[27] Indeed, writes Peirce, "pure theoretical knowledge, or science, has nothing to say concerning practical matters, and nothing even applicable at all to vital crises. Theory is applicable to minor practical affairs; but matters of vital importance must be left to sentiment, that is, to instinct."[28]

This is a paradoxical and dismaying result. But Peirce's instinct is surer than we might think, as Mills himself, more or less unwittingly, indicates. For the practical, from Peirce's point of view, is the "greed philosophy"—"the official common sense philosophy," as Mills writes, "which justified both orthodox Protestantism and the regnant individualism of a growing capitalism and the ideology of wealth."[29]

It is *bourgeois* practice that Peirce recoils from; bourgeois practice, or *praxis*, as we have lately come to say, in the wake of renascent Marxism, still fettering the communitarian forms nascent in science. Hence Peirce's insistence on keeping philosophy "pure." And hence the dilemma, the impossible choice, fettering Peirce's own individual aims, of "business" on the one hand and "monasticism" on the other, philosophy defiled or philosophy spotless. For indeed, there is as yet no suitable praxis for philosophy, which in realizing itself, as Marx wrote, must change the world. (That this praxis, suitable for philosophy, should be *proletarian* praxis, according to Marx, will later trouble Mills greatly as the problem of "historical agency.")

Hence the ambiguity, very troubling to Mills, in Peirce's "laboratory model of mind" as to where precisely mind is "located": inside or outside the investigator; inside, as a "state of mind," an "imaginary laboratory"; or outside, in the real laboratory, together with the test tubes, burners, and so forth. For it is one of the root motives of pragmatism to get mind out of people's heads and into the public world, into the "ensemble of social relations," as Marx wrote, and Dewey also. But the ensemble of social relations is not yet able to sustain mind or sustain thinking about mind. And so the ambiguity stands, declares Mills: "mind or inquiry is in some sense located within or in interaction with the world of physical fact," which is to say, ambiguously located.[30]

Now it is indeed a requirement of action that moves Peirce in his struggle to attain belief, a requirement posed by the collapse, as Henry David Aiken writes, of "the Calvinistic moral agent." It is "a passionate wish to escape from the terrible freedom of one who, as he himself said, had never learned 'moral self-control.' "[31] This is part of the existential meaning, a very Sartrean project, of pragmatism. (And indeed, both Sartre and Peirce share a "search for a method." Sartre writes, concerning "bad faith," a problem familiar to Peirce: "the hypothesis of the Oedipus complex, like the atomic theory, is nothing but an 'experimental idea'; or as Peirce said, it is not to be distinguished from the totality of experiences which it allows to be realized and the results which it enables us to foresee."[32])

"The Calvinistic moral agent *par excellence*," Aiken writes, was William James (1842-1910), an existentialist of sorts (who indeed had an influence on Sartre), and next in the line of pragmatist succession. "In him in fact," writes Aiken, "disbelief always verged upon that final, despairing unbelief which is the paralysis of will. Hence the will to believe; hence also *anything* is meaningful that moves us even for the moment."[33] The main difference between Peirce and James is that James found that the bourgeois praxis, for better or worse, suited him on the whole; and thus where Peirce feared to tread, in "vital affairs," James, though on the side of the angels, precipitously rushed in. In this the James fortune, founded by James' grandfather, a Scotch-Irish immigrant from County Cork, may have played a role.

Thus, where Peirce had scarcely any public, James had many; this gave to his pragmatism its "one single feature," Mills writes: "popularization," or its "orientation to popular publics."[34] About this popularization, Mills, who was later to seek publics avidly, and at last in desperation, is both admiring and scornful: "For James, the "beloved Harvard professor,' living in the midst of many social and intellectual currents, pragmatism was to serve as a 'church' for everyone, and not even a collection was to be taken up."[35] Mills himself gave lectures and addresses before such groups as the Air War College, at Maxwell Air Force Base, the Board of Evangelism and Social Service of the United Church of Canada, and the National Council of the Churches of Christ in the United States of America.

And yet it may be that it was the reclusive Peirce who was the more intrepid adventurer of pragmatism: for while Peirce places his confidence in the community of scientists, and thereby escapes, or hopes to escape, from Calvinism, James, quite without confidence, we may suspect, stubbornly clings to the very Calvinism, more or less, which terrifies him. That is, he continues to seek individual salvation, and to seek it in subjective experience. "The end of life for both the Puritan and the religious liberal of James' variety is individual salvation."[36]

The question of individualism, distinguished from Peirce's collectivism, is at the heart of James' version of pragmatism. In the background, or in James' case in the foreground, is the conflict between religion and science which we have found to be so important in Peirce and the Metaphysical Club. "On the very surface of James' thought," says Mills, "is the major tension of the broad intellectual publics of his day: religion and science."[37]

The resolution which Peirce attempted to effect in a community of belief, at once scientific and religious, is in James deeply personal, deeply private, and as Mills intimates, privatistic: "Religion is a private affair."[38] "Its meaning is for individual ways of life."[39] The "will to believe," consistent with science, is a will to a personally efficacious, personally successful faith. "In James the real locus of pragmatic testing turns out to be a personal and moral sphere."[40]

We may say that while Peirce, in his isolation, looked toward a distant community, James, in the midst of his eager publics, themselves in the midst of the anxieties of bourgeois consolidation, spoke directly to that isolation, to that Peircian crisis of values, and assured everyone, as Justice Holmes wrote, that "everything was all right." Peirce spoke prophetically—and here we should remember Mills' sociolinguistic theory of mind and consider how well it suits these cases—while James meditated and conciliated. Peirce was a visionary, while James, a genuine healer (indeed, a *bona fide* M.D.), applied first aid. "Gradual and in the middle of the road. This is basic to all of James' thinking."[41]

But the deepest current in James' thought is his individualism. And here James draws a little of Mills' fire:

> It is only in the face of immense opposition that thinkers on this continent have advanced against individualism and only by some polemic leverage of note. The lonely Peirce did. The cantankerous and constantly frustrated Abbott did. James did not. Through him flowed urgently the individualism that has been a very central current in American life and thought.[42]

Underpinning James' individualism, apparently, is an ideology of property, which makes ownership, "one of the radical endowments of the race." Here we begin at last to get a sense of Mills as a man of the Left, a sense which his account of Dewey's pragmatism will sharpen considerably:

> In his many contexts James was at bottom conservative. . . . In political matters we have seen that his individualism was bound to place his weight with the regnant laissez-faire attitude. On economic and political questions he was usually in the classic liberal position. He wrote to the dainty Henry that the Chicago anarchists were bound to be foreigners, for no native American would act like that. In a time when the muckrake pack were at a high frenzy he could write that the only motive which "socialistic literature" reckons with is "the fear of poverty if one is lazy."[43]

In his account of the career of John Dewey, still alive and flourishing at the time of the account, Mills wrestles once again with the "problem of thought." And this, as we have seen, is essentially, although rather obscurely, a "locational" problem, a problem of locating thought, "in there," ghostly, locked in the mind, or "out here," in the wide open spaces. What most recommends Dewey to Mills is "the emphasis upon the mundane experiential location" of thought.[44] "The naturalism of instrumental logic displaces thought as the equipment of an absolute self, relativizing it by locating it humanistically as a specific function peculiar to man as an animal trying to get along in an environment."[45] This naturalization of thought and its location, roughly speaking, in the interaction, the active intercourse, of an organism with its environment, is Dewey's "inquiry" or "intelligence."

What this theory accomplishes for Mills, once again, what it does for him, is to offer an escape from the Cartesian trap, the circle of consciousness, and, as Marx wrote, a breakthrough into social action: action, however, which shall be thoughtful action, a unity of thought and action. In this theory also, we are not always thinking, or do not have to be always thinking; we do not dangle from a thread of thought, as in the Cartesian "I think, therefore I am." "Thought arises from antecedent non-reflective conditions."[46] "In the passage from non-reflective to and through reflective modes of experience there is fundamental continuity."[47]

This emphasis on the continuity of the reflective and the nonreflective, and of the origin of the reflective in the nonreflective, also stressed by Peirce ("Inquiry is related to and has its origin within something non-cognitive," )[48] is of especial concern to Mills. It is a rejection of the Cartesian program of methodical doubt, of a radical break with one's settled past, and an affirmation of the integrity of the thinker, through many phases of belief and doubt. It is an affirmation, we may suspect, of the integrity of a conflicted thinker, at odds with himself and his thoughts and beliefs.

But this theory of the location of thought is itself located; it is located sociologically, as we have seen, as a phenomenon of class ascent, demographic shift, professionalization. It is located, finally, in a Great Evasion, as William Appleman Williams has written, the liberal evasion, in brief, of the class struggle and the struggle for political power. As Mills states it:

Underlying and sustaining the cogency of this ethical and metaphysical endeavor is the assumption of a relatively homogenous community which does not harbor any chasms of structure and power not thoroughly ameliorated by discussion. Always there must be the assumption that no "problems" will arise that will be so deep that a third idea-plan would not unite in some way the two conflicting plans. But this model of a problem posing does not concern itself with two social interests in a death-clutch.[49]

For Dewey's first desideratum was unity. What impressed this shy Vermont grocer's son, in his studies at the State University, was the "unity of the living creature": "I was led to desire a world and life that would have the same properties as had the human organism."[50] That this unity is a prime motivation in pragmatism we have already seen. It is the aim at unity, of disunity, of conflict: the will to integrity of a fundamentally conflicted person. It is one of Mills' aims, as we have seen in his essay on China.

When at Johns Hopkins, Dewey came under the influence of George Sylvester Morris, also a Vermont man, who had "reacted strongly against the religious orthodoxy of a Puritan New England upbringing." Through Morris, Dewey began an intensive study of Hegel and was moved most deeply by what he saw as a "demand for unification, " and "intensive emotional craving" (James' own "craving for unity," which was an "aesthetic demand"). And the unity which Dewey found in Hegel was culture: "Hegel's idea of cultural institutions as an 'objective mind' upon which individuals were dependent in the formation of their mental life."[51]

Now the appeal to culture, in this context, is sociologically, among other facets, the liberal evasion itself, the evasion of the division of society into classes. Thus it is that Rousseau, in his bitter attack against class society, most bitterly attacks culture, the "arts and sciences," which constitute the false unity and legitimation of class society. And thus it is that Dewey wrote *Freedom and Culture* late in the Great Depression. The book was not a response to this depression but to the totalitarian societies of Germany and Russia, themselves more developed, more brutal and coercive responses to class antagonism. For culture, we may say, is the mask, the powdered wig of class society (not withstanding Mills' rather different appeal to culture at other junctures).

Dewey writes:

The term culture, thus used, makes for, fits into, or implements, (1) a pluralistic conception of social problems; thus "culture" is an element of a general perspective which would proceed (2) *specifically step-by-step* and (3) which does *not see chasms, irreconcilable antagonisms, between a limited number of empowered structures.* Sociologically, it doubtless has general roots in the essential regionalism of a continental nation, in the diverse structures of various governmental units, and in the extreme heterogeneity of the population of the United States.[52]

These facts of class society Dewey declines to recognize, and it is on this reef that his philosophy of education, the basis of all his philosophy, finally founders. The failure may be seen in the example of Jane Addams' Hull House, a community center for Chicago immigrants, with which Dewey was associated around the turn of the century. For the program of Hull House, of course, was not to abolish classes but to adapt the classes to each other: class cooperation and not class struggle. "Hence," as Mills writes in a footnote, "the problem, the effort, the solution, could be and was put in terms of 'assimilation,'

'Americanization,' or 'democratization.' Thus the 'Immigrant problem,' their 'adjustment' or 'assimilation' to American milieux
obscured the class problem."[53]

This same contradiction, between the pretensions of democracy
and the realities of class society, infects another of Dewey's optimistic
projects, science. For just as we may ask, "Education for what?", we
may ask, as Robert Lynd did, "Knowledge for what?, for what social
purpose?" For science is also adaptational, according to Dewey; it is a
matter of "problems" and not of "values." This Mills calls
"technologism," "the methodization of value;" he comments: "It is
with this standpoint, along with such terms as 'education,' and the
anthropologists' 'culture,' and by varying the level of abstraction, that
Dewey avoids a really definite recognition and statement of the
problem of political power."[54]

Thus, as in Peirce and James, Dewey's pragmatism, or "instrumen-
talism," as he called it, is not a breakthrough into genuine social
action, as Mills conceives it, but an evasion of genuine social action;
once again the great liberal evasion. And it fails, Mills hints at this
beginning of his career, where Marxism succeeds; or at any rate,
Marxism and Deweyism are rival models for social action! "It is
obvious that Marxism as a doctrine and movement has linked practice
and theory; Dewey believes that intelligence or science combines
these two. He wants to deny science and intelligence to Marxism and
he has to admit that it, too, blends action and thought."[55]

To the "absolutism" and "monism" of Marxism, its "monistic
block-universe theory of social causation," Dewey opposes his own
"pluralism," a step–by–step, one–by–one, piece–meal approach to
social problems; and Mills comments: "A monistic theory of causation
is typically calculated for the arousal of mass action: a pluralistic view
approaches political affairs in another manner."[56]

Dewey writes again: "What is needed is specific inquiries into a
multitude of specific structures and interactions." And Mills comments:

Now it is fairly obvious that such inquiry and theories, if the word may be
used here, would not be very well suited for action, e.g., of revolutionary
scale, nor indeed for the large scale planning of a society. It fits into a
conception of many reform movements.[57]

Now there is no doubt that one of the prime motivations of
bourgeois thought, from Hobbes to the present, is to obscure, to
cover up, the brutal realities of class, and to de-fuse the class struggle.

But although Dewey quite properly comes under attack on this point (Henry Aiken speaks of Mills' "terrible indictment"), there lies deep in his thought a very Marxian idea, a Hegelian–Marxian–Darwinian idea, which the undialectical Mills loses sight of: the idea of the totality, the idea that it is society which evolves, like the totality of nature, of which it is a part; society, evolving as a whole, through, as Marx would further insist, contrary to Dewey, class struggle and revolution.

We are indeed very far from an adequate understanding of these matters. All history may indeed, as Marx wrote, be the history of class struggle. But the first premise of all history, Marx also wrote, the living individual, Dewey's own "organism in the environment," is classless. This particular dialectic, of class and classlessness, is never far from Marx's mind, least when he chooses, abortively, to dedicate his great critique of class society, *Das Kapital*, to the naturalist Charles Darwin, a great teacher also of Dewey.

Apparently deeply ingrained in Mills, coexistent with his own emotional and intellectual craving for unity—a "catholic" craving, we may speculate—this matter of class struggle, of which there is already a hint in the 1939 article, will figure prominently in Mills' later life and affords a transition to the next phase of his career, the Labor Phase.

## CHAPTER 3

# *Labor*

IN 1942, while the war raged in Europe and the first phase of his career drew to a close, Mills (rejected by the draft for hypertension) published a review, in the Leftist literary journal *Partisan Review*, of Franz Neumann's Marxist study *The Nazi Behemoth*. The review, a watershed for Mills' later work, is foreboding. It stresses the capitalist underpinning of Nazi Germany, the capitalism not of economic anarchy, as Marx experienced it, but of Weberian total rationalization, "totalitarian monopolistic capitalism." It stresses the roots in this capitalistic economy of Nazi racism and imperialism; it stresses the power of the elites—the monopoly capitalists, the Nazi Party, the state bureaucracy, the armed forces—and the regimentation and fragmentation of the working class. It stresses the "anchorage" of Nazi ideology in "the evolving features of the political—economic structure." And it concludes:

> The analysis of Behemoth casts light upon capitalism in democracies. To the most important task of political analysis Neumann has contributed: if you read him thoroughly, you see the harsh outlines of possible futures close around you. With leftwing thought confused and split and dribbling trivialities, he locates the enemy with a 500 watt glare. And Nazi is only one of his names.
>
> Not only does acceptance or rejection of Neumann's analysis set the type of understanding we have of Germany, it sets our attitude toward given elements in other countries, sights the act of our allegiance, places limits upon our political aspirations: helps us locate the enemy all over the world. That is why Franz Neumann's book is not only the most important to appear about Germany; it is a live contribution to all leftwing thinking today. His book will move all of us into deeper levels of analysis and strategy. It had better: Behemoth is everywhere united.[1]

This behemoth, gathering strength in the depths of American society, struggling toward the light, is the main drift toward fascism, or as Mills prefers to say, "militaristic capitalism," a "corporate form of garrison state." The only force that can stand in its way is labor, the brawny arms of working men and, as we shall see, the brains of the pro–labor intellectuals. This is the force, the power, of democracy against oligarchy (and archetypally, of the sons against the fathers). As Mills writes in an article of 1943, "The chief social power upon which a genuine democracy can rest today is labor."[2]

And let us be clear about it, the enemy is not overseas, but here at home; not an invisible hand, but visible for all to see. The enemy, as Mills writes, is Business, the super-Babbittry of the American Way. As President Coolidge said, not long before the Great Depression, "The business of America is business." "There are structural trends in the political economy of the United States which parallel those of Germany," declares Mills. . . . "The unmistakable economic foundations of a corperative system are being formed in this country by monopoly capitalism and its live political gargoyle, the NAM [National Association of Manufacturers] and its afffiliates."[3] In the light of Watergate and the Indochinese War, one can hardly say that Mills has been refuted.

The power of business must be destroyed, and it must be destroyed at the roots. "The opposition must confront that which gives economic royalists their power within and without government: private ownership of the apparatus of production."[4] This Marxian theme has for Mills the rather im-Marxian significance of blood ties, "family dynasties." "At the top of every country, the executives are blended by blood and interest, by idea and status with propertied families and cliques. In Japan the owning business clans formally adopt their executives as members of the family."[5]

Now the enemy of business oligarchy is labor democracy (also the American Way). This natural enemy of business "must become politically alive." The labor movement must become a political movement, aiming at political power—electorally or otherwise, Mills does not say—and not merely economic gains for labor. "The history of organized business everywhere indicates clearly that it knows its chief enemy to be an independent and political labor movement fructified by pro-labor intellectuals."[6]

Marx believed that by its very nature capitalism would beget its natural enemy; that it would beget this mortal antagonist through its own unconscious laws, expropriating people of their property, making them wage-slaves, concentrating this vast propertyless laboring class in factories, educating them through the industrial process, etc. Thus capitalism would dig its own grave. The failure of this Marxist prophecy—the failure of labor to become a revolutionary force—has bedeviled radical thinkers and organizers for generations. And time is running out, declares Mills. "Unless trade unions unify into an independent political movement and take intelligent action on all important political issues, there is danger that they will be incorporated within a government over which they have little control."[7]

The enemy of business oligarchy, we have said, is labor democracy. But what if there is no labor democracy but only another oligarchy, cooperating with that of business. "Somehow [labor] must become a militant political movement," Mills concludes.[8] Once again, at this crucial juncture, Mills is torn and conflicted, torn between consciousness and life. The consciousness of labor is its leaders, "the new men of power," (a very Weberian motif); its life is the "rank-and-file." Mills does not know where, if anywhere, to place his hopes. Thus:

> When that boatload of wobblies came
> Up to Everett, the sheriff says
> Don't you come no further
> Who the hell's yer leader anyhow?
> *Who's yer leader*
> And them wobblies yelled right back
> *We ain't got no leader*
> *We're all leaders*
> And they kept right on comin'!

But despite this moving affirmation of labor populism (from an interview with an unknown worker, Sutcliffe, Nevada, June, 1947) with which Mills' book opens as an epigraph, it is the labor elite, the "new men of power," that is his subject. Indeed, "The fight against the main drift" depends on the rank-and-file. "The strength of the labor leader is with the rank-and-file; without it there would be no labor leader." And again, "If people show strength, they will find leaders."[9] And yet, dismally, it is on the labor leaders that Mills focuses his expectations: "Never has so much depended upon men who are so ill-prepared and so little inclined to assume the responsibility."[10]

The question in essence, the definitive question of Mills' life, is as he earlier wrote, "Where is the power?" This is a question, it will be seen, closely related to the one with which we began, "Where is the thought?" And if, as it seems, the power is with "the men in power," the prevailing power elite, where is the countervailing power, the power to stop the ominous main drift? Is it in another elite, presently powerless? Is it in the masses? Or is it in the man of knowledge, the lonely thinker, the "pro-labor intellectual?"

In 1942, replying to James Burnham's thesis on managerial revolution, Mills is inclined to answer these questions as a Marxist. The power is with the owners, those who own the means of production. The countervailing power is with the revolutionary masses:

Modern revolutions are not watched by masses as they occur within the palace of elites. Revolutions are less dependent upon managerial personnel and their myths than upon those who bring to focus and legitimate the revolutionary activity of struggling classes. The Russian revolutionaries may have been slight in number, but the peasants who wanted the land were many, and it is they who make revolutionary leaders successful. . . . In modern history always behind the elites and parties there are revolutionary masses. Without such masses, parties may shout revolution, but (no matter how expert they may be) they cannot make it.[11]

Now this question, Who has the power?, is also, since men are mortal, a question of the transfer of power; the question, increasingly to exercise Mills, of "history-making," of historical change. (That historical change is essentially a matter of shifts in political power is a key assumption in Mills which we should not leave unchallenged.) It is archetypally, the question of fathers and sons, the question, as Mills writes, of inheritance, "disposition to the next generation." Indeed, Mills makes this problem of inheritance the crux of socialist revolution:

Socialism begins where a legal order does not provide for succession of property holdings in terms of blood relationship nor for private transfers of power. Hence, in this respect, Nazism stands quite remote from communism. . . . It is by overlooking the problem of inheritance of property that nazism and communism appear as two phases of the same movement. Those who hate the Nazis but fear Russian communism know why.[12]

Thus, as Mills writes in his critique of Burnham, the power in Nazi Germany still rests with the propertied classes, the big industrialists and landowners, and not, as Burnham argues, with the managers and technicians. The prime factor in this controversy, is the rise of the new middle class, which, although technically indispensable to the economy, is still subordinate to the ruling class of property owners. Here we begin to wade knee–deep in the muddy waters of Marxist theory. And indeed, despite his own Marxist point of view, Mills writes here that "Burnham suffers from too much Marx";[13] presumably, from too much "economism," economic determinism.

To be sure, according to one interpretation of Marx (we shall not try here to determine Marx's *ipsissima verba*, which in any case are ambiguous), it is the owners of the means of production, the owners of the farms and factories, that "rule" society. It is from this point of view that Mills faults Burnham initially. But according to another Marxist standpoint, somewhat resembling Burnham's, it is the class that embodies the most developed social energies, the most evolved productive forces, that rules or *comes* to rule; or more broadly, this class takes the lead politically. (The time modalities of power, as we shall see, are of essential importance here.) And what undermines the position of the ruling class and leads, in the present historical epoch, marked by the growth of the proletariat, to fascism, is that this class does not embody the most advanced social energies but continues to rule nevertheless, against the grain of history.

Thus, Mills will later write, in his book *The Marxists*, that Marx's theory of power, is "upset, for example, by the fact of Nazi Germany where, on any reasonable account, parasitical and functionally useless elements of German society gained political power."[14] This is a fundamental misunderstanding of political power. It is the "political illusion," as we may say, which dominates Mills' mind. For fascism rules, which is to say, *usurps* power, holds sway over society by force and without right, as the dictionary says, precisely because it is parasitical and functionally useless. It is the struggle of a dying class to maintain itself in the face of history, in the face of the living, productive forces of history. It is, Marx would insist, as we shall further note shortly, politics in essence. Hence the enormous growth which we are witnessing today the world over of the apparatus of repression and coercion.

Now, can a class "own" without "ruling," or, as is apparently the case in Russia, rule without owning? Mills answers:

There is in Russia no private ownership of the means of production. Nobody owns them. Burnham's assumption that someone must, even if it be managers, because someone "controls" them, is a lag from capitalist ways of thinking. His definition of property as actual disposition means an eternalization of notions of private property.[15]

The problem is indeed, as Mills recognizes, "a political and legal problem." That is, from Marx's point of view, it is unessential, epiphenomenal; for politics and law are mere "forms," more or less illusory, concealing the deeper reality. Moreover, as is not sufficiently clear in Mills, the real problem lies in the transition, which is already taking place, from one kind of society to another; the transition to the future. The bourgeoisie ousts the feudal lords, as the story goes, because they are the "rising class," because they embody the most advanced energies of society—the most advanced praxis, as Marx says. And of course the feudal lords resist and try to hold on to their power. Hence the political struggle, a struggle apparently fought out in the sphere of politics, the sphere of "illusion," but actually engaging deeper economic–productive forces. Thus Marx writes, characteristically denigrating politics, but admitting its provisional necessity:

Revolution as such—the overthrow of the existing power and the dissolution of the old condition—is a political act. But without revolution socialism cannot carry on. Socialism needs this political act insofar as it needs destruction and dissolution. But when its ultimate purpose, its soul emerges, socialism will throw the political husk away.[16]

Thus the question Where is the power? arises primarily in key periods of historical transition, periods when a rising subordinate class locks horns with a declining ruling class. The period Mills is agonizing over, the late bourgeois period, our own period of struggle, should be, according to Marx, a struggle, in the Behemoth which is everywhere, in Nazi Germany and liberal America (hence Mills' scant satisfaction in the Allied victory), between bourgeoisie and proletariat. The agonizing is over the apparent failure of the proletariat to play its expected historical role.

In such a situation—and in any such transitional situation—the question of power is in a sense unanswerable. The owl of Minerva, as Hegel said, flies only at dusk; it is only after the battle is over that we know who won. Thus, to this question Mills has, after all, no answer, but only a kind of swearing and gnashing of teeth: "The question is: Where is the power? And the answer is: It is the structure of domination, which is the state with its monopoly of physical force, and fused within it the industrialists and their agrarian colleagues."[17]

And yet, there are "the new men of power," the labor leaders. We have seen that "business as power" spells fascism. Now if business as power derives its power from private ownership of the means of production, from where does labor derive its power? It is a dark fact of life in America, which augurs ill for socialist prospects in the struggle against fascism, that the leaders of American labor derive their power . . . from American business. For, "Trade unions and private property are now parts of the same system"—indeed incorporated within corporate America; and one of the main functions of the labor leader, and main source of his power, is as a "jobber of labor power." "The labor leader organizes and sells wage workers to the highest bidder on the best terms available. . . . He accepts the general conditions of labor under capitalism and then, as a contracting agent operating within that system, he higgles and bargains over wages, hours, and working conditions for the members of his union."[18]

One of the sources for Mills' study is an article by the Harvard sociologist P.O. Sorokin, "Leaders of Labor and Radical Movements in the United States and Foreign Countries." It is an anomaly of the American labor movement that very few of its leaders have been radicals. At the time Mills wrote his book on labor there was still a scent in the air of the labor radicalism of the 1930's, the time of militant CIO organizing and of bloody strikes. In the election of 1972 organized labor endorsed Nixon, surely a leader of the avant–garde of corporate militarism; and the Communist Party, experiencing a mild renascence, in the wake of the nonlabor radicalism of the 1960's, has changed the name of its newspaper from the well-known *Daily Worker*, to *The Daily World*. As Abbie Hoffman, a radical leader of sorts, said in 1967, at a Socialist Scholar's Conference, "Organize the workers? The workers want to beat the————out of me!"

The decline of the labor movement in America is a complicated story, which requires for its telling a theory of history and a social psychology—both deep concerns of Mills—which we do not yet have. There is help in the work of Wilhelm Reich on "the mass psychology of fascism"—the roots, the "anchorage," as Reich writes, of repressive politics, of political brutality, of rascism, of jingoism, etc.—in broadly speaking, repressed sexuality, will help, as will the studies by Adorno, *et al.*, on "the authoritarian personality." Historical studies of class structure, immigration patterns, consumption patterns, the race question, etc. are also needed. An excellent venture in this direction is S. Aronowitz's recent book *False Promises*.

A sympton of the labor movement's decline is the appearance of a book such as Mills', which reflects the split, between leaders and rank and file, consciousness and life, which is in Marx the root alienation. This is "consciousness emancipated from the world" as elitism, authoritarianism, and imperialism: the social expression, of which history affords abundant examples, of the spiritualistic premise, the spiritualistic, Weberian inversion of the Marxist formula.

In such a situation, foreseeing the main drift, what does a man do? If you are an independent Leftist, a professor of sociology, a one–time pragmatist, and a would-be preacher—if you are C. Wright Mills—you write a book. We have seen how important, in the earliest phases of Mills' intellectual life, is the notion of a "public," the object of a believing subject: a group of people to whom a thinker hopes to communicate his ideas. It is thus that Mills begins his postwar effort to stem the main drift, with an account of the political publics and their relation to the labor leader.

There are, Mills writes, two types of relevant publics, "the small circle of politically alert publics," and "the great American public of politically passive people." Among the politically alert, those who "are keenly and continuously interested in political affairs," there are, in the whole political spectrum, the far Left, the independent Left, the liberal Center, the practical Right, and the sophisticated Conservatives.

The far Left, exclusive of the Communists, is represented primarily by the Trotskyists. Although these forceful, energetic people "want capitalism smashed and socialism, with workers' control, triumphant," they tend, in Mills' estimation, to be narrow and dogmatic. (Mills is not quite the "Texas Trotskyite" some have made him out to be.) "As people of faith, members are dedicated, rationalized, and inflexible; they always have great political will and vast energies, and sometimes a little vision. Given their inconsequent power, they often seem like bureaucrats without a bureaucracy."[19]

The liberal Center is pro-labor, but "the means they would use and the practicality they espouse are short-run and small scale."

As for the Communists, although they have "great zeal and energy," they are—so many charge—undemocratic and unprincipled, and responsive not to the needs of American workers but to "the changing needs of the ruling group in Russia." As the English Marxist, Harold Laski, quoted by Mills, writes:

They have resorted to splitting tactics without any hesitation. . . . Organized as a conspiracy, their major desire is not to select the best possible leadership in ability and character for the end socialism desires; it is to get those upon whom they can count for uncritical and devoted obedience to their orders into the key positions of a movement or party they enter to use for their own purposes.[20]

Unsympathetic to the Trotskyists, the Communists, and the liberal Center, Mills presumably falls, for better or worse, into the camp of the "independent Left."

Like the little magazines which carry their opinions, independent leftists come and go. In a way they are grateful parasites of the left; they seldom attempt organization but can feel strong only when left organizations are going concerns. Because of their lack of organization, they are prone to political helplessness. When events or organizations do not drift their way, they are a powerful third camp of opinion, oscillating between lament and indignation. But when left organizations are on the move, the independent leftists are not without considerable influence. . . . With them political alertness is becoming a contemplative state rather than a spring of action: they are frequently overwhelmed by visions, but they have not organized will. Their expectations are generalized to the point of being moral. Yet they are not simply moralists: they treat political events and trends as symptomatic of the bitter tang and hopeless feeling of current politics. For them the days are evil. But they do not have the organization with which to redeem the time. . . . There is here an almost charismatic wish that man should be enthusiastic and joyous, and the independent leftists do not see how to reconcile this value with such everyday organizations as labor unions, or for that matter, modern industry and government.[21]

Right of center are the practical Right, small business types mostly, who share with the liberals "the same short-run, shifting attention and the same agitated indignation." Finally, there are the sophisticated Conservatives, the power elite itself, "business as power," whose master aim is to make the world safe for American Big Industry. Most important of all, from Mills' point of view, the sophisticated Conservatives "have a program for slump," a program for the periodic economic depressions which have historically afflicted capitalism, and on which Marx placed so much weight. "If the sophisticated conservatives have their way," writes Mills, "the next New Deal will be a war economy rather than a welfare economy . . . a permanent war economy."[22]

Crucial to the strategy of the sophisticated Conservatives is labor. The Right must capture labor for its program of permanent war economy. To do this, the sophisticated Right "would split the labor leader from the rank and file of labor," and "use the leader to manage the working men and women in the unions." (This strategy, writes

Mills, it shares with the far Left, the latter using the leaders to radicalize, the former to de-radicalize, the rank-and-file.) The labor leaders are therefore a "strategic elite," on whom, in "the coming slump," all political forces, right, left and center, will converge. And this is also the main chance for the "pro-labor intellectual," like Mills.

In a slump, there is a question of power and there is a question of intellect. A program would assert how each of the two are to be developed and how ideas and people are to be united into a going concern. The labor leader is now the only possible link between power and the ideas of the politically alert of the left and liberal publics. How will the labor leader behave in the coming slump? That is the key political question for those who want to know what is in the works for American society in the middle of the twentieth century. [23]

From our vantage point twenty-five years later, the strategy of the sophisticated Conservatives may seem to have worked. We have, indeed, a permanent war economy, to which labor seems to be firmly wedded. And what of the coming slump? Here Mills' crystal ball seems to be a little clouded. He predicts both the coming slump and the program for slump. If the program for slump, the permanent war economy, works—if organized labor can be bought off with affluence (there is no question as yet of any moral appeal to labor, any appeal to labor idealism)—all bets are off.

But we can also see that Mills suffers from an excess of pessimism regarding the Conservative strategy; from an insufficiency, perhaps, of far Left Marxist faith—or perhaps merely an insufficiency of Marxist science. For the permanent war economy itself, as Marxists say, and as we read daily in the newspaper, has its "contradictions": repercussions in Europe and the Third World, internal decay in the armed forces, inflation, wide-spread unemployment, the crisis of the dollar, the "energy crisis," pressure at home from blacks, Latins, students, pressure from constitutionalists, conflicts in the ruling class, etc., etc.

The strategy of business-as-power, then, is a permanent war economy, integrating labor within the corporate system. The strategy of Mills . . . is what? Here we return to the notion of "publics" and to large issues of history and historical change. If the strategy of big business succeeds, it is surely not because the leaders of business have managed by force of intellect to win over the leaders of labor. There are, as Marxists say, "objective conditions" making for this strange alliance. What then is the independent Leftist, or any Leftist, to do?

"Political opinions," writes Mills, "trickle from smaller alert publics to the passive mass of the people." But is it, after all, a matter of "opinion"? These are the questions which baffled us at the beginning of our inquiry into Mills, the questions of mind, of belief, of action. As it seems to Mills, at this point, through his book he will influence the politically alert, and through the politically alert affect the mass public, who will in turn influence the labor leader: "The politically alert public which can shape the mass public's interpretation of the slump will thus be the public in the best position to influence the strategy of the Labor leader."[24]

Now the politically alert influence the passive mass in three ways:

First, the liberal and leftward publications, as well as the right-wing newsletters, are read by editors and writers for mass-circulation organs and by radio commentators. The contents of the politically sophisticated media are thus passed on, although in the process they may be sharply restated.

Second, writers for the magazines and papers that serve the politically alert public, graduate, in the typical course of their careers, to better-paying positions with media that serve the mass public. . . .

Third, in their daily lives, the members of the two types of public meet one another, for the politically alert are not socially isolated people; on the contrary, they are the ones who lead what temporary mass organizations exist, and they are the ones who in neighborhood, shop, and office are most likely to initiate serious political discussions.[25]

In these "serious political discussions" we approach somewhat closer to the social theory of mind which Mills is still searching for. But how does he conceive it? His answer: "The politically alert infiltrate the mass public and reveal to its members in face-to-face conversation something of their own political opinions and imagery."[26] Surely the motives on which people are prepared to act—the pragmatist definition of belief, as we will remember—are not formed in this way.

This becomes clearer when Mills turns to other factors in the popular "image of labor," the "mass media of communication and . . . the direct experience which the people have with labor leaders and labor organizations."[27] The mass media, writes Mills, "are not kind to the labor unions or labor leaders." But although the mass media purvey a generally bad image of labor, "The people have experiences which enter into and form their views of labor."[28] "Too many of the people have now been affected by the practical benefits of unionism to accept the negative treatment in the mass media of communication."[29]

The operative word here, a good pragmatist word, is "experience." Here Mills means primarily "personal experience." But there is a historical dimension to experience, perhaps its primary dimension. There is the historical experience of the American people; and this, above all, will be the determining factor, for better or worse, in the American future. As Marx writes, in a passage which Mills is fond of quoting: "Men make their own history, but they do not make it just as they please; they do not make it under circumstances chosen by themselves, but under circumstances directly encountered, given and transmitted from the past."[30]

The historical experience of the present American era, has been above all one of global imperialism, such as the world has not before known. Unlike earlier imperialisms, it is reactionary through and through, a struggle against history, which means the suppression of the material and spiritual aspirations of hundreds of millions around the world. This imperialism and its inseparable partner, domestic oligarchy, have depraved American democracy. Perforce they have depraved the American worker, who has grown fat on the misery of the subject peoples and knows it in his bones. Power corrupts, collectively as well as individually.

As a conservative historian, John Lukacs, coolly, and rather narrowly, writes:

"We have not sought an inch of territory after the last war," said President Eisenhower on several occasions; yet without doubting either the sincerity or the benevolent intentions of this President, it is the historian's duty to point out the necessary qualifications.

In 1945 the United States retained many of the strategic bases and territories which she had taken over during the war in agreement with the other North Atlantic nations: American bases remained in Greenland, Iceland, the Azores. During the cold war, from 1948 onward, the number of American military enclaves and air bases multiplied: in addition to the above-mentioned places in the Atlantic and Carribbean, the United States has acquired, erected, or maintained military enclaves and air bases in Britain, Spain, Italy, Germany, France, Morocco, Libya, Saudi Arabia, Turkey, Greece, South Korea, Japan, Formosa, the Philippines, Vietnam. In addition to these places, the United States has military missions and may use military bases in Norway, Denmark, Holland, Luxembourg, Portugal, Iran, Pakistan, Australia, New Zealand, Siam. Even this list is not quite exclusive: there are a number of other countries where the Unites States maintains missions of a technical nature whose existance is of course, also connected with American national interests.

Despite mutual professions of friendship, offers of Russian alliance, and the dispatch of Russian technical missions to new and unruly nations throughout the Middle East and Africa, up till now not one Russian base has been established beyond the Russian sphere, and no alliance has been concluded with any nation beyond it.

. . . [T]he very extensiveness of this new list of American domains and bases abroad suggests at least the development of a new and not merely temporary conception of American national interests, representing a departure from earlier American traditions. I have already implied . . . how this world-wide extension of American bases and colonies abroad has affected a new American generation, introducing new elements into the historical development of American society and politics.[31]

Thus, as Lukacs writes, "the great transformation of American society," with its "somewhat corruptive delights," indeed, its deadly internal moral rot, "toward an imperial society."[32] Thus, in terms broader and deeper than those of Mills' book on labor, the main drift may be seen as "Shine, Perishing Republic."

What America and American labor need now, if we are going to be free, and play a progressive role in the world, is (to put it somewhat quixotically) rehabilitation. Now there are two ideas, two projects, two traditions, not customarily joined in America, which Mills thinks can rehabilitate America—class struggle and grass-roots democracy; which is to say, industrial democracy, the Jeffersonianism, as Mills writes, of industrial society.

To be sure, Jefferson was not a socialist; the Jeffersonian image is of independent proprietorship, independent farmers and artisans. Nonetheless:

Classic socialism shares its master purpose with classic democracy. The difference between Thomas Jefferson and Karl Marx is a half century of technological change, during which industry replaced agriculture, the large-scale factory replaced the individual workshop, the dependent wage and salary worker replaced the independent proprietor. Left movements have been a series of desperate attempts to uphold the simple values of classic democracy under conditions of giant technology, monopoly capital, and the behemoth state—in short, under the conditions of modern life.[33]

Now, we may agree that Marx carries forward into industrial society the tradition of democracy. But the difference between Jefferson and Marx is not merely a half-century of technological change (although, in Marxist fashion, technological change makes this difference possible). Nor does the Marxist Left struggle simply to uphold the simple values of democracy. It is not, as Mills writes in an article of 1942, because the "independent entrepreneur" has been expropriated that socialism is *necessary*. Rather, it is this expropriation, by big capital, of the independent entrepreneur, that makes socialism *possible*.

The conditions under which private economic enterprise led to independence and freedom in other spheres for the bulk of men was the dominance of an economic system of small proprietorships each based upon self-owned and operated property. These conditions formed the cradle of classic democracy. Under them it is possible to speak of private property and independent work as a basis for political freedom, and for at least a chance at equality. Now these conditions are gone and no nostalgic wish nor reference to Jefferson . . . will ever make shopkeepers out of employees unless we throw away the efficiency of our productive forces.[34]

It is apparent that Mills himself shares this Jeffersonian nostalgia, and that he views, in accordance with the loneliness and apartness of his life ("again I was alone, or at least very much on my own, my own leader")[35] the obsolescence of Jeffersonian man with deep regret. This is to say, that he does not quite yet grasp the idea of socialist man. And indeed the tyranny of kingship is much easier to overthrow than the tyranny of bossism, of behemoth—if, indeed, (enter Max Weber and white collar man), it is at all possible.

There are, writes Marx, three stages in the development of human individuality: patriarchal, bourgeois, and socialist. In the third stage, socialism, individuality based on proprietorship, entrepreneurial individuality, is replaced by "free individuality," "rich individuality." "Free individuality, which is founded on the universal development of individuals and the domination of their communal and social productivity, which has become their social power, is the third stage. The second stage creates the conditions for the third."[36]

Capitalism, let us say, develops the vast world of medical science, in which, however, individuals participate privately, as doctors— entrepreneurs, selling their knowledge and skills—and patients— customers buying the services. The bond between doctor and patients, therefore, which constitutes medical production and consumption, is money. The community is the actual foundation of all production—the collective experience of the race the foundation of medical science—but individuals participate in this world of products on the basis of private property, buying and selling. The social character of medical science, as Marx says, is alienated, and the individuals partaking in it are alienated. "The individuals are subordinated to social production, which exists externally to them, as a sort of fate; but social production is not subordinated to the individuals who manipulate it as their communal capacity."[37]

It thus appears that Mills' "Image of Man"—the title of one of his last books—continues to be a bourgeois image. The image of the entrepreneur or independent craftsman, especially the intellectual entrepreneur with property in his own skills (the academic consultant, for example, able to sell his knowledge to business enterprises), is still highly attractive to him.

The destruction of behemoth, therefore, has for Mills more the significance of restoration, of re-creation, than of creation. In important respects, as we shall see more clearly later, he is a backward-looking man and not, at this point, a dialectical thinker.

Now the destruction of behemoth, as we have noted, means the destruction of oligarchical imperialism. The key to a working oligarchical imperialism is class collaboration, "social harmony"; the key to smashing it is class struggle. And this is where the "liberal rhetoric," the language of cooperation, harmony, of oil on troubled waters, is so dangerous. (Once again, note the theme of language, so important in Mills.)

The liberal rhetoric personalizes and moralizes business-labor relations. It does not talk of any contradiction of interests but of highly placed persons, and of the presence or absence among them of moral traits. Two such traits are stressed: "good will" and "intelligence." If only the spokesmen for both sides were intelligent, then there would be no breach between the interests of the working people and those of the managers of property. If only the spokesmen had enough intelligence to practice the Golden Rule on one another, there would be harmony.[38]

This theme of class struggle appears in Mills' earliest work on pragmatism and sets the tone, as we have seen, for much of his dispute with pragmatism. For example, in 1939: "My conception of the generalized other differs from Mead's in one respect crucial to its usage in the sociology of knowledge: I do not believe . . . that the generalized other incorporates 'the whole society,' but rather that it stands for selected societal segments."[39] Similarly, in an article of 1942, "The Professional Ideology of Social Pathologists," Mills writes:

The "organic" orientation of liberalism has stressed all those social factors which tend toward a harmonious balance of elements. . . . In seeing everything social as continuous process, changes in pace and revolutionary dislocations are missed, or are taken as signs of the "pathological."[40]

From the standpoint of political action, such a view may mean a reformism dealing with masses of detail and furthers a tendency to be apolitical. There can be no bases for points of entry for larger social action in a structureless flux. [41]

The emphasis on class struggle, on the legitimacy, the necessity of class struggle, is superimposed, as we have seen in Mills' early article on China, on a deep attraction to the deepest kind of social harmony. It is the credo of a rebel, who resists his own assimilation, his own incorporation into the whole (hence the stress, in the article on social pathologists, on the "immigrant problem"), and who resists his own deep longing for such assimilation. More precisely, more dialectically, it is the credo of a man, deeply committed to an image of social harmony, of social "catholicity," who will not be fooled; who will not be made conformable to any state of affairs not conformable to that profound image. It is the credo, sometimes of a criminal, a "socio-path," but always of a justice-fighter. It is a credo both catholic and Marxist, because it is collective and class-based, not merely individualistic. It is the credo of a man in conscious revolt against "the norms of an independent middle-class verbally living out Protestant ideals in the small towns of America."[42] Above all, it is the credo, which in Mills ebbs and flows, of a democrat, a radical democrat, with a radical faith in democracy. The "collective dream of the left," which Mills now tries to make manifest, is above all a democratic dream.

What does Mills understand by democracy? "In contrast with the left's dream, formal democracy of twentieth century America is confined to a narrow political area; the rest of man's life, particularly his work, is left out."[43] This distinction between formal, merely political democracy, and living, socialist democracy, between "political emancipation" and "human emancipation," as Marx writes, has a long tradition (and not altogether a happy one, considering the "socialist democracies" of Eastern Europe).

"The perfected political state," Marx writes, "is, by its very nature, the *species life* of man as opposed to his *material life*."[44] In the political state man is one with his species, living the communal life only in the isolation of the voting booth, where he counts only as an integer, one vote, and not as a flesh-and-blood individual. He is a species-being, paradoxically, only for those few moments a year in the voting booth—there he is at one with his fellow man—and then he returns to his material life, his private life, his work, his family, where he lives privately, separately, competitively, in opposition to his fellow man.

This is man's species life as opposed to his material life. The unity of species life and material life, man and citizen, means, among other things, workers' control, power to the people, and direct democracy. Mills writes, "The left would establish a society in which every one vitally affected by a social decision, regardless of its sphere, would have a voice in that decision, and a hand in its administration."[45]

This "participatory democracy"—the SDS rallying cry of the early 1960's—would be deeply educative and humanizing. It would create the new man needed by socialist society. Here Mills forsakes, at least for the moment, Jeffersonian man and looks toward the future: "It is in the workshop, more than in the electoral district, that the new man of a free society must be developed."[46]

These "immense goals" Mills would entrust to the unions: "The unions, in the left's view, should seek to establish a workers' control over the social process of work."[47] This strategy for labor," as Andre Gorz will write sixteen years later, in a book much indebted to Mills, means "that in every workshop or its equivalent the unionized workers would continually strive to encroach upon the functions now performed by owners of industry and their appointed managers."[48] In this strategy, as Gorz writes, of "*progressive* conquest of power," the "union" in Mills' words, "becomes the means of a social revolution in the working life of the worker; it transforms his daily working existence."[49]

Finally, "the left would create an independent labor party to undertake political and economic moves which in daily practice reveal the sovereignty residing in the people."[50]

Now, will this union-made revolution be a revolution from above or a revolution from below? Once again, Mills' position on this crucial issue is deeply infected with ambiguity; an ambiguity, to be sure, intrinsic to the subject matter, to the very notion of a strategy.

To be sure, "In order to proceed with such a program the unions as they now exist would have to be drastically modified at two points: they would have to greatly expand the basis of their membership and they would have to be solidly united."[51] A part of this expansion in union membership would be "the control from below that is the keystone of the democratic aim of the unions."[52] And again, "Those who desire decisive changes in the existing system must stress the transformation of the people from a passive public to an executive organ."[53]

On the other hand: "As the right focuses its program upon the business leader and makes its demands of the business community, so the left focuses upon the labor leader and makes its demands of the laboring community. Business leaders and labor leaders are the two handles which right and left would grasp; they represent the larger groups which these politically alert publics would set in further motion"[54]

And this is where the intellectual comes in. For as we will remember, "There must be the power and there must be the intellect." Labor's strategy is after all executed by a "team of power and ideas"; it is indeed a Grand Strategy. And in the last analysis, as we have seen, it is up to the "strategic elite" of labor leaders to put it into action. "It is the task of the labor leader to allow and to initiate a union of the power and the intellect."[55]

And yet, there is in this last chapter of Mills' book on labor, a view of things quite apart from the sterile premise of the philosopher-king, quite apart from politics as usual; a view which holds out some hope, after all, of stopping the main drift; a view, at long last, of "The People, the People, Yes:", as Carl Sandburg wrote. It is an explosive view, a dangerous view, a vision of elemental power, which once awakened would shatter the present system of labor and labor leaders, business and business leaders. It is a vision of the organization of the vast unorganized; a vision, as Mills writes, of the "underdogs," outside the unions and largely outside society; a vision of many millions, blacks, Puerto Ricans, Chicanos, poor whites, disaffected youth from all classes, etc., who are now, perhaps, on the move at last:

> The condition of the underdog is an important aspect of class relations in America today. The liberal sees it as a problem of "adjustment and participation." Those set against the main drift see it differently: the withdrawn should be remade inside a new kind of union community: then they will be ready to participate. A type of man must be built into a human being outside the present system of society so that he may be able to shake it to its foundations.[56]

And this is no more than the age-old wobbly vision: The Last Shall be First, We Who Are Nothing, We Shall Be All!

I am the people—the mob—the crowd—the mass.
Do you know that all the great work of the world is done through me?
I am the workingman, the inventor, the maker of the world's food and clothes.
I am the audience that witnesses history. The Napoleons come from me and

the Lincolns. They die. And then I send forth more Napoleons and Lincolns.

I am the seed ground. I am a prairie that will stand for much plowing. Terrible storms pass over me. I forget. The best of me is sucked out and wasted. I forget. Everything but Death comes to me and makes me work and give up what I have. And I forget.

Sometimes I growl, shake myself and spatter a few red drops for history to remember. Then—I forget.

When I, the People, learn to remember, when I, the People, use the lessons of yesterday and no longer forget who robbed me last year, who played me for a fool—then there will be no speaker in all the world say the name: "The People," with any fleck of a sneer in his voice and any far-off smile of derision.

The mob—the crowd—the mass—will arrive then.

Carl Sandburg

# CHAPTER 4

# White Collar

I F the ultimate vision of *The New Men of Power*—an admittedly quixotic vision—is of "The People, Yes!", the masses triumphant, the underlying vision of *White Collar*, three Cold War years later, is of the masses eternally submissive, and the main drift triumphant. It is a vision, as Orwell wrote (and Mills, during these years, was much concerned with Orwell), of a foot stamping on a human face forever—but a face indifferent to being stamped on. It is a vision of "a society in which men are the managed personnel of a garrison state."[1] It is a vision, as Herbert Marcuse will later write—acknowledging "the vital importance" of Mills—of a "society without opposition," "nonterroristic totalitarianism," totalitarianism through manipulation of needs.[2]

"The labor leaders and the U.S. workers," wrote Mills in 1948, "are not alone if they choose to fight. They have potential allies of pivotal importance." These potential allies are the middle classes, and most hopefully, "white collar people." "All those who suffer the results of irresponsible social decisions, and who hold a disproportionately small share of the values available to man in modern society are potential members of the left."[3] "The program of the left, if realized in time, can stop the main drift only if it succeeds in counter-organization among these middle-class elements."[4]

In 1951 the Left and its collective dream have vanished in the high noon of the Cold War; unionism has become a bad dream; and the New Left of the 1960's is a gleam in no one's eye. The alliance of white collar workers and wage workers, which Mills called for earlier, now means only "a unionization into the main drift."

The story of labor in the Franklin Roosevelt era encouraged hope because labor was then emerging for the first time on any American scale; it had little need of any sense of direction other than to "organize the unorganized." But in Truman's Fair Deal this is not the case: not the mandate of the slump, but the farmer's fear that his enormous property might be taken away from him; not millions of unemployed, but labor's fear that Taft-Hartley acts will be used against existing unions are the underpinnings of this administration. Then thought of war was not dominant, and men of power could pay serious attention to the distribution of domestic power; now fear of war hangs over all political speculation and deadens the political will for new domestic beginnings.[5]

Mills' *White Collar*, ostensibly a study of social stratification, is in essence an American epic. It is a mid-century story, with its counterparts in many works of literature—Mills cites Booth Tarkington's *Alice Adams*, Christopher Morley's *Kitty Foyle*, and Arthur Miller's *Death of a Salesman*. It tells of the "decline of the free entrepreneur and the rise of the dependent employee on the American scene . . . the decline of the independent individual and the rise of the little man in the American mind."[6] Its hero, a true mid-century hero, is "the white collar man" (although Mills' own fictional citations refer more often to women.) This white collar man, as Mills writes,

. . . is more often pitiful than tragic, as he is seen collectively, fighting personal inflation, living out in slow misery his yearning for the quick American climb. He is pushed by forces beyond his control, pulled into movements he does not understand; he gets into situations in which his is the most helpless position. The white collar man is the hero as victim, the small creature who is acted upon but who does not act, who works along unnoticed in somebody's office or store, never talking loud, never talking back, never taking a stand.[7]

In the beginning, as the story goes, was the small entrepreneur, and above all, the rural entrepreneur. In this "scattering of farmers," of men of "absolute individualism," neither peasants nor aristocrats, lies the root of the American experience. "Europe's five-hundred-year struggle out of feudalism has not absorbed the energies of the United States producer; a contractual society began here almost *de nova* as a capitalist order."[8] (Slavery, "the glaring exception to the more generous ideals of the American Revolution," did not loom as large as is often assumed.[9])

This absolute individual, the masterless individual, supremely, heroically independent, a propertied individual who "owned the sphere of his own work,"[10] looms large in Mills' imagination. To this extent we can call it a liberal imagination; but on a more personal level, we can recognize the imagination of a man from an early age "painfully isolated," who early embarked on "the search for absolute autonomy."[11] This is the fallen, the vanquished hero, the liberal hero, the free, the self-reliant one, the craftsman. This is the ruling archetype of Mills' life and work. As Mills recognizes, he is a tragic hero, who sets in motion the forces that will destroy not only him, but liberal man and liberal society. For he is, or must soon become—and here lies Mills' profound ambivalence—a capitalist, a business man: "A free man, not a man exploited, an independent man, not a man bound by tradition, here confronted a continent and, grappling with it, turned it into a million commodities."[12]

Thus, following on the American farmer, who, as Mills writes, "has always been a real-estate speculator as well as a husbandman,"[13] is the business man. "Here, if anywhere," says Mills, "the small capitalist had his rural chance."[14]

The world of small entrepreneurs was "self-balancing." It was the competitive world of self-regulating capitalism, extolled by the classic theorists and ideologues of capitalism. "Within it no central authority allocated materials and ordered men to specified tasks, and the course of its history was the unintended consequence of many scattered wills each acting freely."[15] A crucial aspect of this world was, as the Constitution stipulates, "The right of the people to keep and bear arms": "decentralization of the military order," as Mills writes; or as he liked to say, "One man, one gun."

This capitalist order was not only an economic order, but a moral order; it defined, as we have said, an image of man:

Competition was a means of producing free individuals, a testing field for heroes; in its terms men lived the legend of the self-reliant individual. In every area of life, liberals have imagined independent individuals freely competing so that merit might win and character develop: in the free contractual marriage, the Protestant church, the voluntary association, the democratic state with its competitive party system as well as on the economic market. Competition was the way liberalism would integrate its historic era; it was also a central feature of the classic liberal's style of life.[16]

This world of self-reliant men—so the implicit dialectic of Mills' argument goes—already bears within itself its antithesis, the white collar class. It bears within itself the seeds of its own destruction—above all, the seed of false consciousness, which is one of the great themes of Mills' work, and which grows into the submission of the people to their own oppression. For the "ideal of universal small property held those without property in collective check while it lured them on as individuals."[17] Individuals did not organize against property, because each hoped to become a propertied individual himself.

In the end, the development of the split between small and large property, rather than any sharp red line between those with property and those without it, destroyed the world of the small entrepreneur. Yet the historical fulfillment of the big enterpriser was hampered and delayed for long decades of the nineteenth century. The smaller world was sheltered by international distance, and if what was to destroy it already lay within it, the small entrepreneur in his heyday was not made anxious by this emerging fact about the society he was so confidently building. Between mercantilism and subsistence farming in the beginning, and monopoly and high finance at the end, the society of the small entrepreneur flourished and became the seedbed of middle-class ideal and aspiration and myth.[18]

The next chapter of the story, then, is "the transformation of property," the expropriation of small property—"democratic property," as Mills writes—and the growth of "class property"—business as power. At this point, Mills borrows from a commentator in the midst of the small entrepreneur's epoch, John Taylor. This transformation of property is indeed an invasion of property, not sudden and violent, like insurrection, dividing the property of the few among the many, but slow, gradual, and legal, transferring the property of the many to the few. As such, it defines the course of American history.

Its first, and according to Mills, its most important phase, is the "rural debacle," the expropriation of the farmer: "Insofar as the vision of the classic economic liberalism was realized in America, it worked itself out on the family farm."[19] But the family farm is fast becoming a thing of the past, and where it exists it is likely to exist in illiteracy and malnutrition: "Within the rural populace, the market mechanics and technological motors of social change have been cutting down the proportions of free enterprisers."[20]

Unlike the small farmer, the small businessman "has never formed a broad stratum which, like the rural, could enact a key role in the shaping of a free society."[21] From the beginning, he has been dependent on bigger men, for raw materials, capital, outlets to markets, etc. He has a very high rate of failure, and despite his continuing great numbers, mostly in the retail and service industries, he "has been deprived of his old entrepreneurial function."

At the bottom of the entrepreneurial world is the "lumpen bourgeoisie," the proprietors of "family businesses," where the owner and his family do all the work. These "midget entrepreneurs," consumed by "competitive anxieties and family tensions," are a far cry from the masterless enterpriser of earlier days, whom George Sorel characterized, in Mills' words as "a class of serious moral habits, filled with its own dignity, having the energy and will to govern a country without a centralized bureaucracy."[22]

The spirit of the lumpen bourgeoisie is mean, petty, calculating, repressive. "It is, . . . as Wilhelm Reich has noted, a feature of such petty-bourgeois life that extreme repression is often exercised in its patriarchal orbit."[23] (The reference to Reich, an early follower of Freud, and an early and great "Freudo-Marxist," who earned much notoriety for his unorthodox ideas, betrays an important influence which Mills seems generally to wish to conceal.)

Since there is little or no outlet for feelings beyond the confines of the shop or farm, members of these families may grow greedy for gain. The whole force of their nature is brought to bear upon trivial affairs which absorb their attention and shape their character. . . . The family circle is closed in and often withdrawn into itself, thus encouraging strong intimacies and close-up hatreds. The children of such families are often the objects upon which parental frustrations are projected. They are subjected alternately to overindulgence, which springs from close parental competition for their attention, and to strong discipline, which is based on the parents' urge to "make the child amount to something." . . . There is evidence that the coming to adolescence of the lumpen-bourgeois child is a painful juncture frought with many perils for parent and child, and perhaps also for society.[24] (This passage bespeaks firsthand observation. Mills' father held a position in Goldstein's Store in Waco, Texas, until 1923.)[25]

We may suspect that this is a rather sharp bifurcation of virtues and vices: the freedom, independence and self-reliance of the liberal hero, the propertied democrat, extolled by Mills in passage after passage; the protofascist meanness and cupidity of the lumpen bourgeoisie. For do not all these bourgeois types—and let us use the word "bourgeois," which Mills carefully avoids in most contexts— live from property (Marx's criterion of class, and hence of class "psychology" or character); and do not all of them live for gain, i.e., seek to capitalize on what they own, although, to be sure, the vast variety of businesses conditions a vast variety of character types among businessmen? Indeed, the lumpen bourgeoisie, according to Mills' account, should be more and not less free, less independent, and less self-reliant than their more affluent confreres; and their property should be more and not less democratic; for what defines them as lumpen, distinguishing them from the other middle-class elements, is that they employ no labor. In Mills' words, "The true lumpenbourgeoisie . . . employ no workers at all."[26]

To be sure, bourgeois individuality—an individuality based on property—was in its day a rich and salutary growth. It is the foundation of the great world of bourgeois culture. But as Marx insists, it is a narrow individuality, broader than the feudal type, but narrower than the socialist because its basis in human *association*, human togetherness, is narrower. (We do not, indeed, need Marx to make this point. For Mills has already debunked bourgeois individuality in his book on pragmatism, where it is the "greed philosophy" which Peirce revolted against and James embraced, the philosophy which makes "ownership," as James wrote, "one of the radical endowments of the race.")[27]

And what is the basis in human association of Mills' free, independent entrepreneur? "He was an 'absolute individual,' linked into a system with no authoritarian center, but held together by countless, free, shrewd transactions."[28] Mills surely sees the crassness of this kind of individual and this kind of social solidarity—the crassness of this image of man—but he is nonetheless strongly attracted by it.

Now it is true that if you have an "independent income," you are in the straightforward sense freer to do as you like than if you have to sell your labor. This, indeed, is part of Marx's critique of bourgeois "freedom." But the question is not so simple, and independence not so clear and absolute a value; for the whole system of nature is one of *interdependence*, and this interdependence is raised to the highest degree in human society, *social* nature, and finally consummated, according to Marx, in socialism. Thus Durkheim, the French-Jewish collectivist (also a strong individualist, in a dialectic which eludes Mills), "was convinced," as A. Kardiner and E. Preble write, "that the social interdependence of individuals was the reality and the true glory of human life, and he applied his own extraordinary independence to the scientific foundation and application of that principle."[29]

In the world of "absolute individuals," held together by "countless, free transactions," many are ruined by the smallest circumstance. The condition of real independence, and really free individuality, is not free competition, which presupposes the separation of men from one another, but the regulation of social production by associated men and women: the subordination of social production, as Marx writes, "to the individuals who manipulate it as their communal capacity."[30] The individual is free, according to Marx, only as a "universal" individual, as a species-being, in solidarity with his species. He is free only to the degree that "he makes the community his object." And he makes the community his object above all in associated labor—labor based not on private property, however "democratic," but on communal property.

Mills is familiar with these pages of Marx, as his extensive account of white collar "alienation" indicates, but he continues to extoll the old entrepreneur, the "unalienated" small capitalist. In this respect Mills joins in the "rhetoric of competition" which he ostensibly decries. But whatever the old entrepreneur was in the past, he is surely, as Mills insists, no model for the future: "Over the last hundred years, the United States has been transformed from a nation of small capitalists into a nation of hired employees; but the ideology suitable for the nation of small capitalists persists, as if that small-propertied world were still a going concern."[31]

Nor does anyone any longer really want competition. The farmer has become dependent on government price supports and subsidies, and "It is a narrowed upper stratum of businesslike, politically alert farmers who are flourishing, not a world of small entrepreneurs."[32] No longer is farming a "morally ascendant way of life."[33] The small businessman, less successful than the farmers, is overpowered, politically and economically; the big firms who overpower him use him ideologically to advance their interests. Squeezed by big business, the small businessman nevertheless identifies with it and turns his aggression toward labor and government, "Big business exploits in its own interests the very anxieties it has created for small business."[34]

The situation, ominously, somewhat resembles that of pre-Hitler Germany, where the Nazis were able to use the frustrations of small business, created primarily by economic concentration, against labor and the Weimar democracy. As Mills warns once again, "Many of the problems to which Nazism provided one kind of solution have by no means been solved in America."[35]

Although the "old middle classes are still the chief anchors of the old American way, and the old way is still strong,"[36] the trend is toward greater and greater concentration of property. From the point of view of the past, the point of view of classic democracy, as Mills understands it, and the all-important view of "independence," this is a downward trend: "The distribution of man's independence, in so far as it is rooted in the ownership and control of his means of livelihood and his equality of power in the market, is thus drastically narrowed."[37] From the point of view of the (socialist) future, which Mills also adopts, the trend is progressive: " 'Middle-class radicalism' in the United States has been in truth reactionary, for it could be realized and maintained only if production were kept small-scale."[38]

Political freedom can no longer be rooted in ownership; for as we have seen, we have become a nation of employees, dependent on huge concentrations of property. And for the few owners of those properties, freedom means "freedom to do what one wishes to the freedom and security of thousands of dependent employees."[39] In the future, therefore—in what must be called a dictate of prudential socialism, rather than of any socialist image of man—the struggle for freedom, far from being a struggle for small property, in the tradition of "progressivism," must be a struggle "against the institution of property itself."[40] It must be, in the spirit, somewhat muted now, of Mills' earlier book on labor, a struggle for workers' control: "For the employees, freedom and security, both political and economic, can no longer rest upon individual independence in the old sense. To be free and to be secure is to have an effective control over that upon which one is dependent: the job within the centralized enterprise."[41]

Thus there has arisen "the white collar mass"—propertyless people who comprise over half the members of the American middle class as a whole. Unlike craftsmen, so much admired by Mills, white collar people do not live by making things: "rather, they live off the social machineries that organize and coordinate the people who do make things. . . . [T]heir characteristic skills involve the handling of paper and money and people."[42]

In terms of property, "they are in exactly the same property-class as the wage-workers."[43] They have none. They are "propertyless dependents"—a category, as we have seen, which causes Mills, striving for "absolute autonomy," much anxiety. In terms of social stratification—and here Mills has a bone to pick with Marx, for whom property, as Mills understands it, was the sole stratifier—they form a stratum of their own. They have, of course, different occupations than wage-workers; that is what defines them as white collar. They earn more money than wage-workers, enjoy greater prestige, and exercise greater power. "White-collar employees are the assistants of authority; the power they exercise is a derived power, but they do exercise it."[44]

The main reason for the growth of the white collar mass has been the steady growth of bureaucracy. This sounds a theme of the utmost importance to Mills; the theme, originating in Max Weber, of bureaucratization, routinization, the inexorable drift, made indispensable by dictates of efficiency, toward the wasteland of total administration: the drift, which, there can be no doubt, Mills views with horror, toward the cheerful robot. This is the managerial demiurge, the rise to power, in every sphere of life, of managers and of "the managerial type of man."[45]

In the ten years since he reviewed James Burnham's book, *The Managerial Revolution,* Mills has given further thought to the question of the relationship of power and property, the all-important question, as we have seen, of Who has the power? His position continues to be highly ambiguous: "There is no doubt that managers of big business have replaced captains of industry as the ostensibly central figures in modern capitalism . . . the entrepreneurial function has been bureaucratized."[46] But these bureaucrats continue to derive their power from personal ownership of property. "If the powerful officials of U.S. corporations do not derive their power from personal ownership," states Mills, "their power is nevertheless contingent upon their control of property."[47]

This argument is still not clear. If there is, as Mills admits, "a division between 'ownership' and 'control' of property," and if "control" means "power," who has power over whom and what? Do the controllers control the owners, and if not, why not? Indeed, it often seems as if it is the enterprise itself that has the power: "the Enterprise itself comes in time to seem autonomous, with a motive of its own: to manipulate the world in order to make a profit. . . . Just as the working man no longer owns the machine but is controlled by it, so the middle-class man no longer owns the enterprise but is controlled by it."[48] Thus, as Marx so often writes, the motor of capitalism is not the personal greed of the capitalist: "Capital is not a personal, it is a social power." "The capitalist himself only holds power as the personification of capital."

Indeed, this whole question of power, although it touches on the essence of Mills' thought, is analyzed, following an essentially Weberian scheme, in only the most cursory way. "Coercion," Mills tells us, is "the ultimate type of power," and "involves the use of physical force by the power-holder." "Authority involves the more or less voluntary obedience of the less powerful. . . . Manipulation is a secret or impersonal exercise of power; the one who is influenced is not explicitly told what to do but is nevertheless subject to the will of another."[49]

A crucial complication in the theory of power is "the movement from authority to manipulation," where "the victim does not recognize his status." Here power is exercised over people without their knowledge. Neither coerced nor consenting, they obey; they do what the power-holders want, without knowing it. The countervailing power against this insidious power by manipulation, interestingly enough, is not reason or arms, but, as we later discover, *feeling*. This affectional dimension of life, usually suppressed by Mills in favor of volitional models—decision-making, for example—becomes of the utmost importance in Mills' later theory and therapy of our white collar malaise.

The essentially bourgeois orientation of Mills' thought is nowhere more evident than in his treatment of the fate, in the white–collar world, of the "free professionals of the old middle class."[50] For example, "the self-sufficiency of the entrepreneurial physician has been undermined in all but its economic and ideological aspects by his dependence, on the one hand, upon technical equipment that is formally centralized, and on the other, upon informal organizations that secure and maintain his practice."[51]

We noted in the previous chapter the reactionary character of "entrepreneurial medicine," and the necessity, in line with scientific and social progress, of "socializing" medicine. This socialization, bringing together, alongside complex technical apparatus, all kinds of scattered, self-sufficient practitioners (like the scattered Jeffersonian farmers), becomes itself a new force of medical production. For among the forces of production, Marx writes, are "the modes of cooperation."

Hence the appearance in recent years of the "health commune," and of "community medicine." These are labor pools of medical personnel—doctors, nurses, technicians, paraprofessionals—who associate democratically to serve the health needs of local populations. In this trend, in the increased dependence of medical practitioners on a variety of personnel and on a complex technology, the "independent man" extolled by Mills, is indeed expropriated; but this dependence is an organic part of the development of social production and secures for the "dependent" individual an enriched and more powerful existence.

The legal profession offers a similar example. There have developed not only the "legal factories," serving the rich, which Mills was already acquainted with, but "law communes" which take the place of the independent entrepreneur to practice poverty law, civil liberties law, consumer law, landlord-tenant law, "community law." This is a vast extension, a broadening and not a narrowing, of the scope of the legal profession and of its opportunities for individual development. It is part of the movement, unforeseen by Mills, to make law serve the people.

It is in the universities and among nonuniversity intellectuals—in Mills' own sphere—that the fate of the independent man is most problematical. Here independence means primarily "independence of mind," which academic life tends at all times to militate against. (This bold distinction between true and false intellect goes far back in Mills' career as a loner and rebel. Elected to Phi Beta Kappa at Texas, Mills refused to accept his key and wrote asking that his name be removed from the list of initiates: "Membership is based on points made in a system of grading that is grossly inadequate and crudely inaccurate. Inadequate in its selection of traits which are used in evaluating who are thinking and who are not."[52]

The graduate school is often organized as a "feudal" system: The student trades his loyalty to one professor for protection against other professors. The personable young man, willing to learn quickly the thought-ways of others, may succeed as readily or even more readily than the truly original mind in intensive contact with the world of learning. The man who is willing to be apprenticed to some professor is more useful to him.[53]

After he is established in a college, it is unlikely that the professor's milieu and resources are the kind that will facilitate, much less create, independence of mind. He is a member of a petty hierarchy, almost completely closed in by its middle-class environment and its segregation of intellectual from social life. In such a hierarchy, mediocrity makes its own rules and sets its own image of success. And the path of ascent is as likely to be administrative duty as creative work.[54]

In analogy to the economy, academic men may be producers, who create ideas—predominantly "individual entrepreneurs"; wholesalers, who distribute ideas in textbooks; or retailers, who teach students. All academic men also consume ideas, but some specialize in consumption and "are great on bibliographies."

"In the twentieth century," Mills asserts, "academic life in America has by and large failed to make ambitious men contented with simply academic careers."[55] Hence the opening up of "careers of a new entrepreneurial type": consultants to business and government, the setting up of research institutes, etc. "Yet there is evidence, here and there, even among the youngest men in the greatest hurry, that these new careers, while lifting them out of the academic rut, may have dropped them into something which in its way is at least as unsatisfactory." What academic life lacks above all is political engagement. "This vacuum means that the American scholar's situation allows him to take up the new practicality—in effect to become a political tool—without any shift of political ideology and with little political guilt."[56]

It is evident that Mills is not, as another radical, Paul Goodman, once characterized himself, a "loyal university man"; that he does not think highly of academic life; that as a theorist of mind, he finds it, paradoxically, mindless. It is significant that Mills gives not the slightest hint of any awareness that a different organization of academic life, especially a different relationship between teachers and students, might break up the pattern of producing, wholesaling, retailing, consuming ideas, and make for a genuine knowledge-process, genuine politically active dialogue, inside and outside the classroom; that a reorganization of the university might make it truly minded and politically engaged; that this dense concentration of teachers and students, the "knowledge factory," is, like the industrial factories of an earlier era, politically volatile, with revolutionary potential.

Thus Mills is taken quite by surprise, a few years after *White Collar*—along with most others, to be sure—by what, in his famous "Letter to the New Left", he calls "the young intelligentsia." As Carl Oglesby wrote in 1969, six years after Mills' death:

. . . when a lonely and doubtless very brave American radical, C. Wright Mills, began to put political pieces together in a political way, he could hardly have guessed how quickly—a matter of half a decade?—a rising generation would move to refute one of his cardinal political observations. Refute: for even through the remarkable moral and physical energy which sustained him, one could not fail to understand that Mills saw himself as a political desperado whose most difficult struggle was against a very persuasive despair. The first and continuing need of those whom his polemic would bring to activism would be to prove the possibility of what he considered next to impossible, a radical movement with some serious power behind it.[57]

While the Professors are discussed along with the Doctors and the Lawyers, the Intellectuals, "Brains, Inc.," are given a chapter of their own. They are, writes Mills, the most far-flung and heterogeneous of white collar groups. They can be defined not as a single social unity, but only "in terms of their function and their subjective characteristics. . . ." They are "people who specialize in symbols" and as such, "produce, distribute, and preserve distinct forms of consciousness."[58]

The intellectuals, ideally, are free, self-sufficient men *par excellence*. In the words of William Phillips, quoted by Mills, they have been in "recoil from the practices and values of society toward some form of self-sufficiency, be it moral, or physical, or merely historical, with repeated fresh starts from the bohemian underground as each new movement runs itself out. . . ."[59] As specifically political intellectuals, writes Mills, "they create, facilitate, and criticize the beliefs and ideas that support or attack ruling classes, institutions and policies; or they divert attention from these structures of power and from those who command and benefit from them as going concerns."[60]

But the "conditions of freedom" are no longer available for the free intellectual, any more than for his partner the free entrepreneur, with whom his fate is coupled. As Mills recounts it, his career in this century has gone through four major transformations, until at last he has been reduced, as Mills painfully and awkwardly puts it, to "the malaise of a spiritual void."[61] In view of Mills' own ceaseless struggle to define himself as an intellectual, it is worth reviewing his account of this history.

Before the First World War, in the heyday of pragmatism, the typical intellectual was either a radical muckraker, "who individually sought out the facts of injustice and corruption and reported them to the middle class,"[62] or a member of the conservative elite, of the type of Henry Adams, "who also were critical of crass capitalism, but in a gentlemanly manner, from the standpoint of the patrician rentier."[63]

In the postwar 1920's, the era of Mencken and Sinclair Lewis, intellectuals acquired "an apolitical tone, or a cultivated relaxation into a soft kind of liberalism, which relieved political tension and dulled political perception."

In the 1930's, when Mills himself came to maturity, "there was a widespread model of the intellectual as political agent." A "fashionable Marxism" sprang up to replace the declining pragmatism which was earlier "the nerve of leftward thinking." "One idea runs through both ideologies: the optimistic faith in man's rationality." Many intellectuals, following Lenin, believed themselves the heroic vanguard of the revolution, supplementing the proletarian masses. Some few joined the labor movement, where, if they became firmly attached, Mills writes, they ceased to be intellectuals: "For a time, all live intellectual work was derived from leftward circles or spent its energy defending itself against left views."[64]

The 1940's, the years of Mills' starting out, began with the war. "Intellectuals broke with the old radicalism and became in one way or another liberals and patriots, or gave up politics altogether." These were years of "religious obscurantism," "totalitarian liberalism," and "war ideology." "Few intellectuals arose to protest against the war on political or moral grounds, and the prosperity after the war, in which intellectuals shared, was for them a time of moral slump."[65] A "new metaphysics" arose, to justify "the process of rationalization"—the very process which is the subject of Mills' book. The seeds of the white collar class were definitively laid.

The postwar years came to reap the harvest. Kierkegaard and Kafka, analysts of personal tragedy and hopeless bafflement, replaced Dewey and Marx: "the optimistic, rational faith has obviously been losing out in competition with more tragic views of political and personal life."[66] Dewey's brave words, "Every thinker puts some portion of an apparently stable world in peril," have been forgotten. And Mills is no longer a Marxist.

This "political failure of intellectual nerve" has sociological under-pinnings. The same process of rationalization, bureaucratization, depersonalization, that has created the new middle class in business and professional life, "increasingly sets the conditions of intellectual life and controls the major market for its products."[67] The free intellectual, the intellectual craftsman, has become an employee, a dependent salaried worker. Like the free entrepreneur, he has been expropriated. Nor is he able any longer to communicate his knowledge freely; for although "he lives by communication," he has been expropriated of the means of communication. "Between the intellectual and his potential public stand technical, economic, and social structures which are owned and operated by others."[68]

Nor does the university offer much refuge for independent intellect; for the professor, as we have seen, is an employee, inhibited by his dependent position and by the norms of academic "discretion" and "good judgment."

Nonetheless, intellectuals need not be idle. It is a function of the intellectual to produce and disseminate symbols of justification and diversion; to produce suitable myths legitimating bureaucratic society and allaying the middle-class fears and anxieties attendant upon the recurrent crises of bureaucratic society. And since in bureaucratic society decisions of social policy are made irresponsibly by the few at the top, a great number of intellectually equipped men and women are needed, inside and outside the bureaucracies, to mislead, deceive, and placate the public. The intellectual, in short, has become, as Mills writes, a mouth piece. In the years since *White Collar*, the years of Eisenhower, Kennedy, Johnson, Nixon and Ford, years of crisis in the Western world, such deception has been practiced on an increasingly wide scale (e.g., Watergate), and a subsidiary industry has grown up to expose it.

Thus the intellectual has ceased in many cases to be a free intellectual, asserts Mills, and "has joined the expanding world of those who live off ideas as administrator, idea-man, and good-will technician."[69] He has become, above all, "a man with a job in a society where money is supreme," Mills charges: "No longer, in Matthew Josephson's language, 'detached from the spirit of immediate gain,' no longer having a 'sense of being disinterested,' the intellectual is becoming a technician, an idea-man, rather than one who resists the environment, preserves the individual type, and defends himself from death-by-adaptation."[70]

This is not the vision of mind, of man as a minded organism, which Mills learned from pragmatism. It is not the vital organism, invoked against the main drift, in biologic and esthetic images reminiscent of Dewey, that is here at work, making and remaking a world where vitality can flourish. It is a vision, once again, of the waste land:

> The independent artist and intellectual are among the few remaining personalities presumably equipped to resist and to fight the stereotyping and consequent death of genuinely lively things. Fresh perception now involves the capacity to unmask and smash the stereotypes of vision and intellect with which modern communications swamp us. The worlds of mass-art and mass-thought are increasingly geared to the demands of power. That is why it is in politics that some intellectuals feel the need for solidarity and for a fulcrum. If the thinker does not relate himself to the value of truth in political struggle, he cannot responsibly cope with the whole of life experience.[71]

It is this "truth in political struggle" that intellectuals have increasingly withdrawn from: they lack, Mills writes, "political will." In the face of defeat and powerlessness, they escape into alienation, or, if they are social scientists, into the "cult of objectivity." In both cases, they evince the definitive white collar anxiety; "the political psychology of the scared employee."

For an intellectual like Mills, trying to situate himself socially, for the sake of both action and reflection, this question of "the social role of the man of knowledge," as Mills liked to say, borrowing from Mannheim and Znaniecki, is of pivotal importance. It is, as we have seen, at the root of Mills' first intellectual work, his struggle to formulate a "social theory of mind," and it continues to preoccupy him in his study of pragmatism. By the time he comes to write *White Collar*, the question has become one of deepening crisis. Once again, "The malaise of the American intellectual is . . . the malaise of a spiritual void."[72]

In 1939, Walter Benjamin, in an article paralleling the work of Mills, called "The Author as Producer," attempted to situate the question of intellectual work "in the living social context." Like Mills, who aims to understand "the creation and diffusion of ideas and moods . . . as social and historical phenomena"[73] Benjamin, with greater Marxist rigor, attempts to locate intellectual work within the process of material production itself: "This question aims directly at the function that the work has within the literary relationships of production of a period."[74]

Thus Benjamin is able to expose the roots of the intellectual's malaise and also point toward its resolution. For in considering the author as producer, we are to re-examine the fundamental contradiction in the bourgeois intellectual production process, the contradiction which Mills has furiously been beating his wings against: "the separation between author and reader."[75]

The impetus for Benjamin's critique comes largely from Berthold Brecht, a figure much admired by Mills. ". . . [I]n politics," writes Benjamin, "it is not individual thoughts, but as Brecht once expressed it, the art of thinking what is in the heads of other people, that is decisive."[76] Here is Mills' social theory of mind, here is the key to the problem of preaching, of changing people's minds! Mills has from the start misconstrued his situation and the role of the intellectual in the class struggle.

What maintains the bourgeois order, from the point of view of intellectual work, from the point of view of "communication," as Mills writes, is that very notion of the public, going back to the earliest essays, that defines Mills' life work. And what maintains this notion of the public—consumers who are not producers—is the bourgeois "cultural apparatus." Benjamin writes: the actual publication process—books, articles, lectures. This publication process must be transformed, as Brecht transformed the theater, "transforming the functional relation between the stage and the public, text and production, director and actor."[77] It must be transformed, especially, in the way that the Soviets, according to Benjamin, transformed the newspaper in the 1920's:

In the Soviet press, the difference between author and public, maintained artificially by the bourgeois press, is beginning to disappear. The reader is indeed always ready to become a writer, that is to say, someone who describes or even who proscribes. As an expert—even if not a professional, but only a job-occupant—he gains entrance to authorship. Labor itself speaks out, for writing it out in words constitutes part of the knowledge necessary to becoming an author. Literary competence is no longer based on specialized training in academic schools, but on technical and commercial training in trade schools and thus becomes common property. In a word, it is the literalization [sic] of the relationships of life which overcomes otherwise insoluble antinomies and it is the showplace of the unrestrained degradation of the word—that is, the newspaper—which prepares its salvation.[78]

To be sure, the cultural apparatus, as Benjamin writes, by and large belongs to capital, and where it does not belong to capital, tends, as Marcuse has shown, to be subverted by it. And yet Brecht's plays, in analogous circumstances, were written and performed. This is the lesson of the "counter culture," the struggle, not unknown to Mills ("Letter to the New Left," *Listen Yankee*), for new forms, new techniques, carrying forward a cultural revolution which perhaps is the crux of revolution in our time. It is, in cultural terms, the piecemeal revolution which Mills advocated for labor. Thus, says Benjamin, the necessity for intellectuals always "to think through, in a revolutionary way, their own work and its relationship to the means of production, its productive techniques, its technology."[79]

More important than this, however, is the classroom. Benjamin was not a teacher, and Mills was an unhappy one (although, as his students will attest, energetic and often "exhilarating"). But it is in the classroom, above all, in the knowledge factories, in teaching-and-learning (for example, in the endlessly prolonged tutelage of the dreary system of graduate "training") that the intellectual production process must be transformed. This Mills seems not to have realized. But Benjamin intuits it:

An author who teaches a writer nothing, teaches nobody anything. The determinant factor is the exemplary character of a production that enables it, first, to lead other producers to this production, and secondly to present them with an improved apparatus for their use. And this apparatus is better to the degree that it leads consumers to production, in short that it is capable of making co-workers out of readers or spectators.[80]

The topic of alienation, the question of What is the trouble?, which has been so widely discussed since the late 1940's, takes essentially two forms in Mills. One concept, already discussed at length, stresses the social psychology of job-dependence and sets Mills somewhat apart from Marx, for whom the image of independent life is a mere "Robinsonade," after Robinson Crusoe. (But Marx did call for the abolition of wage labor.) The other, which links Mills closely to Marx, is the concept of the Great Salesroom, and of the Personality Market: the prevalence, in every sphere of life, of "the commodity form," as Marx wrote; of the "cash-nexus," of buying-and-selling. As Mills writes: "This is a time of venality: In the world of the small entrepreneur, selling was one activity among many, limited in scope, technique, and manner. In the new society, selling is a pervasive activity, unlimited in scope and ruthless in choice of technique and manner."

This venality, however, is not a matter for moralizing. It depends, as Marxists say, on objective conditions, namely, the capitalist imperative to market the goods turned out in such huge quantities. "In the twentieth century, as surpluses pile up, the need has been for distribution to national markets; and with the spread of national advertising, co-extensive sales organizations have been needed to cash in on its effects."

Thus the manipulation which Mills characterizes as the most insidious form of power, is, as Marcuse will emphasize a few years later, the manipulation of needs. "High pressure selling is a substitute stimulator of demand, not by lowering prices but by creating new wants and more urgent desires,"[81]

It is indeed, on the question of needs, the possibility of a distinction between true needs and false, real needs and artificial needs, that Marxism stands or falls. It is the hope of Marxists that underneath false consciousness lies real need; that while the mind can be endlessly deceived, the body sooner or later speaks the truth. This is why it is so important to Marx to insist that life determines consciousness and not consciousness life, and why the Weberian exception to this thesis, an exception which Mills tends to embrace is so damaging to Marxism.

It must be remembered that the same process which produces false consciousness, at the same time produces the new and real needs that will refute false consciousness. For as the productive forces develop, the human body, as Spinoza wrote, becomes more and more "fitted for many things." As Andre Gorz writes, "capitalist affluence clearly gives rise to needs that it cannot satisfy and that may assume an explosive character. . . . These needs, however, are no longer mainly quantitative ones; they tend to become qualitative; they are mainly the need to find some satisfaction and some meaning in the work being done."[82] He continues by pointing out that "empirical sociologists," Mills among them, "tend to question the existence of these new and higher needs."[83] They tend to doubt, that is, that there is any limit to manipulation. And indeed, sociology itself is in many respects the very science of manipulation.

Nonetheless, there is in Mills' soul an image of creative work. It is the humanist image, going back to the Renaissance, the "exuberant" image, of work as craftsmanship. It is an essentially esthetic image, which finds its image in Dewey and Mead, as well as in Marx:

> Craftsmanship, as a fully idealized model of work gratification, involves six major features: There is no ulterior motive in work other than the product being made and the processes of its creation. The details of the daily work are meaningful because they are not detached in the worker's mind from the product of the work. The worker is free to control his own working action. The craftsman is thus able to learn from his work; and to use and develop his capacities and skills in its prosecution. There is no split of work and play, or work and culture. The craftsman's way of livelihood determines and infuses his entire mode of living. . . . His work is a poem in action. He is at work and at play in the same act.[84]

And yet Mills does not believe in this image, which is so dear to him. For he writes, "work has no intrinsic meaning."[85] And it is, in any case, a bourgeois image, an entrepreneurial image, which is to say, in Marx's terms, "monadic"; it is an image, once again, of independence and self-sufficiency, an image of the single man, and not, as in Marx, of "the free and pleasurable relationships among human beings." (Thus Marx writes: "The morality of the world we live in takes care not to call work the free and pleasurable relationships among human beings.")[86] Finally, the image is irrelevant . . . just an image. Life today is not, cannot be, like that.

> . . . if the work white-collar people do is not connected with its resultant product, and if there is no intrinsic connection between work and the rest of their life, then they must accept their work as meaningless in itself, perform it with more or less disgruntlement, and seek meanings elsewhere.[87]

These meanings white collar people seek in "leisure." The sadness
and compassion with which the outwardly hard-boiled Mills approaches his white collar people is nowhere more evident than in this
slice of life:

Each day men sell little pieces of themselves in order to try to buy them back
each night and week end with the coin of "fun." With amusement, with love,
with movies, with vicarious intimacy, they pull themselves into some sort of
whole again, and now they are different men. Thus, the cycle of work and
leisure gives rise to two quite different images of self: the everyday image,
based on work, and the holiday image, based upon leisure. The holiday image
is often heavily tinged with aspired-to and dreamed-of features and is, of
course, fed by mass-media personalities and happenings. . . . The weekend,
having nothing in common with the working week, lifts men and women out
of the gray level tone of everyday work life, and forms a standard with which
the working life is contrasted.[88]

What is the fate of the white collar people? In the Great Salesroom,
in the society of the Personality Market, their fate is not a happy one,
and bodes ill for American democracy. Differentiated from the lower
strata most conspicuously by the clothes they wear, their work-a-day
appearances, their vaunted white collars, deeply involved in prestige
striving, always on the edge of a status panic, their self-esteem
perpetually in jeopardy, "they open themselves to a precarious
psychological life."

And it is psychology that is at stake here. It is psychology that steps
between consciousness and life and produces false consciousness,
undermining the foundations both of liberalism and Marxism. This is,
above all, the psychology, unrecognized by Marx, so Mills would
argue, of status, of emulation, of envy; the psychology of conspicuous
consumption, so astutely delineated by Mills' mentor Thorstein
Veblen—stultifying patterns of consumption, which, in the Affluent
Society, even among the nonaffluent, become the negative of social
praxis, the Achilles heel of Marxist expectations. This stumbling
block to the Marxists is "the grand problem of the psychology of social
strata."

Now as Mills seems to forget, Veblen himself, in an observation of
pivotal importance, speculated that socialism would resolve this
problem:

Under a regime which should allow no inequality of acquisition or of income,
this form of emulation, which is due to the possibility of inequality, would

also tend to become obsolete. With the abolition of private property, the characteristic of human nature which now finds its exercise in this form of emulation, should logically find exercise in other, perhaps nobler and socially more servicable, activities; it is at any rate not easy to imagine it running into any line of action more futile or less worthy of human effort. [89]

And indeed, Marx himself has already said that "the positive overcoming of private property," as distinguished from its not yet positive overcoming, "crude communism" (apparently, in Marx's mind, a theoretical construct, and not, as some have supposed, a historical reality), is definitively the overcoming of envy: "The thought of every piece of private property as such is at the very least turned against richer private property as envy and the desire to level so that envy and the desire to level in fact constitute the essence of competition." [90]

How is this "supersession of private property," as Marx writes, the supersession, essentially, of envy, accomplished? Here again is the issue dividing Marx's historical materialism from all forms, as it were, of historical spiritualism; from the "German ideology," as Marx writes. For private property is positively overcome, and communism established, as "the solution of the riddle of history," not, in the first instance, through the alteration of consciousness, but rather, as Veblen also seems to postulate, through "the real movement of things"; i.e., the economic process, the dynamic of production and consumption, working itself out. Just as private property did not arise through the alteration of consciousness (as Weber, indeed, argued), but as "the *sensuous* manifestation of the movement of all previous production," so will it lapse through the "*material, sensuous, . . .* movement . . . of *actual* life"; through the material movement of human self-realization in history, "the realization or actuality of man." [91] (Note the sensuous, material, communitarian forms of the "counter culture" in the immediate historical era.)

And yet, at least for the theorist of consciousness, the riddle of history remains. (There may be a solution for the theorist of "unconsciousness," of the deep, but by no means fatalistic, unconscious movement of history, of which, as we shall see, Rosa Luxemburg is a leading proponent.) As Mills continues, two "models of political consciousness" are available to us: the liberal model of the "alert citizen," informed of his rights and consciously acting to promote his political interest; and the Marxian model, an "ingenious" one, "which reaches from gross material conditions, anchored in property, into the inner consciousness of men of similar class positions." The liberal model is based on a "woefully utopian, rational psychology, which might make sense in a simpler democratic set-up but was impossible in modern society."[92] The Marxian model is similarly flawed by a rationalist assumption, declares Mills. "Both Marxism and liberalism make the same rationalist assumption that men, given the opportunity, will naturally come to political consciousness of interest, of self or of class."[93]

Neither Marxism nor liberalism take account of "political indifference." "Yet such indifference is the major sign of both the impasse of liberalism and the collapse of socialist hopes. It is also at the heart of the political malaise of our times."[94]

It is surely only a psychology of the irrational, a psychology, in this sense, of stupidity, that can give an account of that strange phenomenon Mills calls political indifference, that reef on which many democrats and socialists have run aground. Such a psychology Freud gives us; and Wilhelm Reich, elaborating and modifying Freud's theory in his *Mass Psychology of Fascism,* provides one of the best accounts of this political aberration, and of its close relative, which Mills does not touch on here, popular reaction. The psychology of political indifference is the psychology of instinctual repression. Mills, who is acquainted with Reich's work and draws on it in his account of the "lumpen bourgeoisie," does not follow him here.

In fact, Mills has already dismissed contemptuously the Freudo-Marxian premise put forward by Reich, in an exchange with Paul Goodman, as "the gonad theory of revolution," evincing a shocking brutality toward the most precious sphere of human life. (What else should revolution be? What else *could* revolution be?) It is this theme of the body and of Eros—as Goodman writes, some years before Marcuse—of somatism and anti-somatism, that is at the heart of the controversy dividing Marxian materialism and Weberian, more generally, religious, immaterialism or spiritualism. It is at the heart, also, of the controversy between "economism," as Lenin wrote, and politics; for economics of course is the sphere of bodily gratification (or nongratification), whereas politics, the political illusion, the sphere not of *need* but of *will*, and as such bitterly denigrated by Marx, is the spiritualism, the anti-somatism, of social life. Thus Mills writes:

For a long time conservatives have stressed the biological immutability of man's nature, whereas progressives have emphasized the social plasticity of his character structure. Conservatives have tried to buttress every status quo by appealing to the biological instincts of man. Now Paul Goodman seeks to overturn a particular status quo by appealing to the apparently same instinctual nature.[95]

And Goodman replies, with a far sounder grasp of the present political significance of so-called "instinct theory":

Then is it the fact that radicals—not "progressives"—have emphasized the plasticity of original nature rather than cried out precisely against the outrages against it? I need not mention the anarchists and utopian socialists who have drawn on the French revolutionary word Fraternity, the eros that creates institutions. But is it so sure that Marx and Engels believed that there was no original nature or that it was unimportant? Is it not their position that we must destroy class institutions just in order that true humanity, with its tragedies, can assert itself?[96]

On the other hand, is it not just the fascists—not the "conservatives"—who have most relied on the notion that by fear, repression, and coordination a man can be made to conform to any symbols whatever? I am not implying that the authors are fascists, but that they are indeed progressives—not radicals. I wonder, however, since we are not to speak of inherited powers and their realization and cultural perfection, exactly on what do these progressives base their "humane scheme of values"? *Where do they find the motives for their Sociolatry?*

Where indeed? Thus Mills writes in a characteristic sociological evasion of real *motivation*,—motive *force*, originative, generative, indeed, genital, or in D.H. Lawrence's terms, "sexual-alimentary," a unity of the economic and the erotic:

Freedom does have as its condition specifiable institutional arrangements. But its locus is not between man's biological impulses and institutions. In all societies of which we know, these impulses are structured and defined in their content by whatever values prevail for given men. Men in society learn to will what is objectively required for the enactment of institutionalized roles. And values and slogans legitimize these roles and the trained impulses which sustain their enactment. Freedom lies in choice of roles being open to individuals and to classes of individuals. Its locus is the institutional arrangement of these roles, not the absence of conflict between biologically given drives and the structure of institutions.[97]

Where in this sociological evasion—an evasion, in the last analysis, of the sensate human body—is freedom to find a foothold when all is "institutionalization"? And what is this freedom which "lies in choice of roles"? The foggy verbiage conceals a deep anxiety.

Thus Mills, under the sway of role theory and the political illusion is hard put to give an account not only of political indifference but of politics itself as an autonomous sphere of social praxis. Marx, as we have seen, thought politics—power relationships, the authority of one man over another—was epiphenomenal and would disappear after the socialist revolution in favor of "free human production" in "free and pleasurable relationships among human beings." Nevertheless, in Mills' account of political indifference there is an important clue to the problem of our political malaise; the alienation, as Goodman writes, of "man's consciousness from his nature." For political indifference, Mills who never voted in a national election emphasizes, is not necessarily irrational, not necessarily a defect of reason; "in fact, it may be a reasoned cynicism, which distrusts and debunks all available political loyalties and hopes as lack of sophistication."[98]

In fact, as Mills struggles to make clear, it is as much a defect of *feeling* as of *reason* (which is to say, that an adequate theory of politics requires a theory of mind which does not admit these conventional distinctions between reason, feeling, and other human powers). It is, as Mills observed it during the Second World War, on the home front, a "sort of numbness"; there were "no chords of feeling;" "no mainspring of feeling was let loose in despair or furor." "It was a time of somnambulance." "There were no plain targets of revolt; and the cold metropolitan manner had so entered the soul of overpowered men that they were made completely private and blasé, down deep and for good."[99]

There was, in fact—and this is the essence of the matter, despite Mills' appeal to rational calculi of personal interest—no *social* feeling. "Some time after World War I, American democracy, no longer a widespread confidence and an authentic social feeling, became an objective for official propaganda. It became official and conventional."[100]

As Mills already knows from his Catholicism, now presumably left far behind, and from Peirce's pragmatism, also receding into the distance, the species *exists*, the real is the community; and this community is one as much of feeling as of reason; or rather, because it is a community, it harbors no distinction between reason and feeling. But the American reality, which is an unreality—hence the numbness, the sleepwalking—is not the community. It is, as Mills says, privatism: "If we accept the Greek's definition of the idiot as a privatized man, then we must conclude that the U.S. citizenry is now largely composed of idiots."[101]

As an urban specialist, Herbert Gans, has noted (I paraphrase) "The big mistake planners make is to try to plan for community. People don't want community. They want privacy, they want the detached suburban house, the private garage, the T.V." And (outside the purview of Gans, the "cultural relativist") they are miserable. As Mills writes:

> The image of success and its individuated psychology are the most lively aspects of popular culture and the greatest diversion from politics. Virtually all the images of popular culture are concerned with individuals, and more, with particular kinds of individuals succeeding by individual ways to individual goals. Fiction and non-fiction, movies and radio—indeed almost every aspect of contemporary mass communication—accentuate *individual* success. Whatever is done is done by individual effort, and if a group is involved, it strings along after the extraordinary leader. There is displayed no upward climb of and by collective action to political goals, but individuals succeeding, by strictly personal efforts in a hostile environment, to personal economic and erotic goals.[102]

Now the answer to idiot privatism is not idiot collectivism; it is not a different line in the mass media. Privatism, as Marcuse has emphasized, is of the body. Because the sensate body is a species-body—we have the body of our species, a human body—privatism renders that body insensitive. The antidote to privatism is to re-sensitize the body: and to re-sensitize it, first of all, to pain. White collar people are miserable, Mills emphasizes. They must come alive to their misery.

The first breakthrough from political numbness to political feeling came with the freedom rides and sit-ins of the late 1950's and early 1960's, the time of Mills' rising influence, and his "Letter to the New Left": long bus rides from north to south, blacks and whites together, and most of them middle-class; deprivation, brutality, beatings, blood. A similar phenomenon of this era is the upheaval in the Roman Catholic Church under Pope John: also an awakening to pain—the poor, the Jews—which has left in its wake, among other effects, the many married priests and nuns; an awakening to pleasure, the sensate body. What has to be done, as Thomas Paine wrote, is to provoke "people to think, by making them feel; and when once the veil begins to rend, it admits not of repair."[103]

Now ten years of war in Indochina seem to have heavily anesthetized America once again (much of America at least; for many, like Paine, still keep the faith). How there may by another awakening is anybody's guess. "This is a bureaucratized society of privatized men, and it may very well go along in this condition for a long time to come."[104] (A few years after Mills wrote this came the breakthrough I speak of.) What is the fate of the white collar people? Apathetic, manipulated, privatized, deadened, preoccupied with their dreams of private success, they are, Mills writes, "up for sale: whoever seems respectable enough, strong enough, can probably have them. So far, nobody has made a serious bid."[105] That was written in 1951. Today, after Nixon's 1972 landslide, Mills might conclude his book differently.

## CHAPTER 5

# The Power Elite

MILLS' fourth book, *The Power Elite*, was published in 1959, at the close of the Eisenhower era. These were airless, arid, sex-starved years; hysterical, hydrogen-bomb, McCarthyite years; plague years, as Stefan Kanfer has recently written; years not of social struggle, ghetto uprisings, student unrest, the troubles of the 1960's, but rather years of the ad man, apathy, conformity (all daily decried in the higher-brow media); years whose troubled underside surfaced in San Francisco in 1956, in Allen Ginsberg's "Howl": "Moloch! Solitude! Filth! Ugliness! Ashcans and unattainable dollars! Children screaming under the stairways! Boys sobbing in armies! Old men weeping in the parks! Moloch! Moloch! Nightmare of Moloch! Moloch the loveless! Mental Moloch! Moloch the heavy judger of man!" Moloch years, indeed, but nonetheless "peaceful," curiously complacent, looked back on nostalgically by some.

In words redolently Millsiane (at a 1951 *Partisan Review* Symposium, "Our Country and Our Culture," in which Mills also participated), Norman Mailer protested

A symposium of this sort I find shocking. . . . This period smacks of healthy manifestoes. Everywhere the American writer is being dunned to become healthy, to integrate himself, to eschew disease, to revalue institutions. Is there nothing to remind us that the writer does not need to be integrated into his society, and often works best in opposition to it? . . . Today, the enemy is vague, the work seems done, the audience more sophisticated than the writer. Society has been rationalized, and the expert encroaches upon the writer. Belief in the efficacy of attacking his society has been lost, but nothing has replaced the need for attack. . . . Really, the history of the twentieth century seems made to be ignored. No one of the intellectuals who find themselves now in the American grain ever discuss—at least in print—the

89

needs of modern war. One does not ever say that total war and the total war economy predicate a total regimentation of thought. . . . One never hears about the disappearance of the world market, nor is it polite to suggest that the prosperity of America depends upon the production of means of destruction, and it is not only the Soviet Union which is driven toward war as an answer to insoluble problems.[1]

In the mixture of complacency and Cold War hysteria, apathy and inner terror, which characterized those Eisenhower years, there were three key ideas: (1) that someone was in charge and everything was all right; (2) that no one was in charge and everything was all wrong; and (3) the most sinister hypothesis, that someone was in charge and everything was all right for them, but all wrong for the rest of us. It is, of course, the third hypothesis that is Mills'. The "someone in charge" is the power elite.

Now the power elite wears many faces. But the simplest of these greets us at the very beginning of Mills' book; it is that of our old friend, the free and independent entrepreneur: "The powers of ordinary men are circumscribed by the everyday world in which they live, yet even in these rounds of job, family, and neighborhood, they often seem driven by forces they can neither understand nor govern. 'Great changes' are beyond their control, but affect their conduct and outlook nonetheless. . . . The power elite is composed of men whose positions enable them to transcend the ordinary environments of ordinary men and women; they are in positions to make decisions having major consequences."[2]

The bad seed of property has produced a monstrous growth: the bigger fish have devoured the smaller; free competition has produced monopoly; the scatter of free entrepreneurs has produced the concentrated, malevolent might of a few. And this, as Mills discerns only fitfully, is part of the inner logic of the very institution of free property which so captivates his mind.This is privatism,the privatism, in the first instance, of the property-holder, the man whose labor is based on private property, the independent craftsman. The power elite is the bad conscience, the nightmare, of this independent craftsman. Through privatism, which, as Mills discerns, still fitfully, is the root alienation, species-alienation, and in this sense, as Marx wrote, through alienated labor,

. . . man thus not only produces his relationship to the object and to the act of production as an alien man at enmity with him. He also creates the relation in which other men stand to his production and product, and the relation in which he stands to these other men. . . . As he alienates his own activity from himself, he confers upon the stranger an activity which is not his own.[3]

Thus there is both a subjective and an objective dynamic in the power elite. What is the evidence for the existence of this "compact and powerful elite of great importance [which] does now prevail in America"? It is, subjectively, the dread of nuclear holocaust; objectively, and without any social psychological nuances—a matter, however, of great scientific importance to Mills—the real possibility of nuclear holocaust. Thus it is "the domination of the military event" that primarily points to the power elite. And indeed, as Daniel Bell observes, Mills' image of power, and of politics generally, is essentially one of violence. This is "one man, one rifle," the military side of independent craftsmanship. From this point of view, the power elite is a Cold War fantasy. Objectively, however, the power elite is historically real. The independent craftsman does become monopoly capitalism, which becomes oligarchy and imperialism.

Once again, it is as an outgrowth of the Jeffersonian economy, of the "great scatter of small productive units in autonomous balance," that the power elite has arisen—as an outgrowth, normal or pathological, of "the autonomous play of market forces":

When numerous small entrepreneurs made up the economy . . . many of them could fail and the consequences still remain local; political and military authorities did not intervene. But now, given political expectations and military commitments, can they afford to allow key units of the private corporate economy to break down in slump? Increasingly, they do intervene in economic affairs, and as they do, the controlling decisions in each order are inspected by agents of the other two, and economic, military, and political structures are interlocked.[4]

This is a thesis fairly congruent with Marxism: the need to maintain a permanent war economy, to surmount the periodic crises of capitalism. But as Mills takes pains to emphasize, the power elite is more than the impersonal power of monopoly capitalism. The Millsian theory, unlike the Marxist, is a theory of "the powerful": a social-psychological and not merely a sociological theory. It is—although Mills would probably deny this—a Hobbesian theory. "So that in the first place," Hobbes wrote, "I put it for a general inclination of all mankind, a perpetual and restless desire of power after power, that ceaseth only in Death."[5]

This is why Mills finds the Jeffersonian scatter so attractive. "By the powerful," Mills writes, following Weber, "we mean, of course, those who are able to realize their will, even if others resist it."[6] In the Jeffersonian scatter, the desire of power for power is dissipated in the open spaces. In denser concentrations of people, it runs up against human resistance, if only the resistance of men occupying space, and becomes a power over other men.

This is a theory of human powers and inclinations markedly different from Marx's. That very scatter of independent farmers, which for Mills is the basis of free individuality and free democracy, Marx describes as "the idiocy of rural life": the great obstacle to class consciousness and class politics, and the very soil, not of freedom, but of despotism. Indeed, as an ideology—the ideology of small property, which as Mills emphasizes in *White Collar*, has survived its sociological reality—it is the very basis of the power elite:

The small-holding peasants [small property owners] form a vast mass, the members of which live in similar conditions but without entering into manifold relations with one another. Their mode of production isolates them from one another instead of bringing them into mutual intercourse. . . . Each individual peasant family is almost self-sufficient [independent]; it itself directly produces the major part of its consumption and thus acquires its means of life more through exchange with nature than in intercourse with society. . . . The political influence of the small-holding peasants [small property owners], therefore, finds its final expression in the executive power subordinating society to itself [the power elite].[7]

Here Mills directly, although only implicitly, joins issue with Marx on the question of power. For Marx, power is precisely the power of "mutual intercourse," of combined strength. The powerful are precisely those who "enter into manifold relations with one another," relations which are not "power relations," in the conventional parlance; not a "zero sum" game, where one man's power gain is the other man's power loss. The dictionary defines "power," in the first instance, as "the ability or capacity to act or perform effectively." Let us asume that this means "to realize one's will." Is the single man, Robinson Crusoe, since there is no one to resist his will, pre-eminently powerful? Indeed, he lives like a king, with his massive capital, his possessions, animals, etc. Is he more or less powerful after the advent of the man Friday, the other man who may resist his will? And if Friday makes him more powerful, is it in his capacity as a companion or as a servant, a man *in* his power?

The dictionary continues:"Powerful": having, or capable of exerting, great (moral, physical, or other) power: potent: having power to influence greatly." In none of these cases does "powerful" have the primary sense of having one's way, getting what one wants. Rather, it means producing a good effect, as in "the power to heal." In this Spinozistic idea of power, a powerful person is one who can evoke power in another person, make him stronger and not weaker; who can affirm the other's power, the other's ability to act or perform effectively.

A similar distortion infects Mills' notion of politics itself. "All politics," writes Mills, following Weber, "is a struggle for power; the ultimate kind of power is violence." "Why," Mills wonders, "is not military dictatorship the normal and usual form of government?"[8]

Now in the primary sense, as Aristotle wrote, politics is simply the organization of a polity, a human community, formed in and by nature—for man is a social animal—to satisfy the needs, both material and spiritual, of this animal. And this, as Paul Goodman has pointed out, is the opinion even of Machiavelli, the high priest of *Realpolitik*. For Machiavelli simply says what is self-evident, that the aim of politics is the public welfare—indeed, the public happiness, as John Adams wrote. As the American Declaration of Independence suggests, in terms quite opaque to Weber, the unhappy sociologist, and incidently, the people, even in mobs, storming through the streets, are far superior in glory and goodness to princes.

Thus, contrary to Weber, and in accordance with the humanist tradition which Mills so often invokes, the "state," or more generally, as Weber writes, "political association," "human community," does indeed have a humane end proper to it. It is not to be defined, as Weber defines it, solely in terms of its means—"physical force"— although this may ultimately be indispensable. It is not and cannot be, conceptually or otherwise, not even in Orwellian terms, simply "a relation of men dominating men," "a structure of domination," "a compulsory association which organizes domination." ("I state," writes Weber, "only the purely *conceptual* aspect for our considera- tion: the modern state is a compulsory association which organizes domination.")[9] For even in the politics of 1984, there are interests served, which are not simply the interest in "power," domination, i.e., *material*, economic interests, which are the indispensable humanism of politics. Always, it is not merely, as Weber believes, "the distribution of power" that is at stake—this is the perfect unreality, the idealism, the utopia, of *Realpolitik*—but the distribution of *goods*. Indeed, even political power, according to its concept (*polis, virtu*), can be given a Spinozistic (and Platonic) definition: *viz.*, the power to evoke power in the citizenry, to help them to be better men and women. This subordination, and effective, existential, denial in the dialectic of spirit and matter, of material need—abstractly, the "economic sphere"—in favor of religious motives, is of course the crucial issue underlying all of Weber's work. (We may speculate that this bespeaks, in conjunction with Weber's *Realpolitik*, a profound anxiety about material need and the situation of dependency it enforces.)

Nonetheless, it is true that this aim of politics is realized only through political struggle, and sometimes armed struggle, especially in class society. In fact I am inclined to believe, it is true in any society, for any society, continually generating "separated" classes, as Mao has realized, Michel's "iron law of oligarchy" and its implicit corrolary, the "iron law of democracy," will always be in constant strife. Thus Jefferson wrote, in a somewhat sanguinary vein, that "The tree of liberty must be watered every twenty years with the blood of patriots": a maxim, in less sanguinary terms, presupposed by our own constitution of checks and balances.

But this struggle, this "struggle for power," as Mills writes, is clearly not the principle of politics, not its *raison d'être*, but a means by which society is organized and reorganized, to the greater or lesser advantage of the common welfare. And this is why military dictatorship, although it has the preponderance of power, in Mills' terms, is not the normal form of government. For the military as such has no politics on which to form a government. It is, in Weber's terms, a "status group," the status group *par excellence*, with its essentially feudal "status honor," its rank and hierarchy, superordination and subordination; but it is not a class, which, rooted in the economic process, at the nerve centers of production and consumption, can become a "ruling class." Thus violence, either repressive or revolutionary, is in this sense only the means of an ulterior political end, either of a special class or, as "armed struggle," of the popular majority or their representatives. This question of "the mob," "the crowd in history," and "armed struggle" will be exceedingly important in our later consideration of Mills' theory of democratic politics and "the mass society." As Machiavelli writes:

Now, someone might say that such proceedings were unusual and almost inhuman—to see the people assemble and cry out against the Senate, the Senate cry out against the people, to see the people storm through the streets, shops shut down, all the plebs march out of Rome—things frightening even to read about. I say that all cities must have devices by which the people can demonstrate their concern and interest, especially those cities which intend to engage the people in important undertakings. Among other devices Rome had these: when the people wanted a law enacted they behaved as I have described or they refused to enlist for the wars. Consequently, in order to placate them it was necessary to satisfy their wishes in some way; and the wishes of free people are seldom damaging to freedom, for they grow out of oppression or the fear of being oppressed.[10]

To be sure, there are power relations in society; there are those who command and those who obey; those, it would appear, who rule and those who are ruled. At the family dinner table—the household on which Aristotle based all political community—it is the father, and not the child, who may say, "There shall be no soup-slurping at this table." And yet we must say that at the heart of this power there is a mystery. Precisely how do the powerful "realize their will," and how is the obedience of those subjected to it exacted? Weber asks: "When and why do men obey? Upon what inner justification and upon what external means does this domination rest?"[11] He does not really answer. But Rousseau, who puzzled over the same mystery, has already said, with deeper insight, "It is very difficult to reduce to obedience one who does not seek command; and the most adroit politician would never succeed in subjecting men who wanted only to be free."[12]

At this point in his argument Mills introduces another puzzling idea, that of "institutions." It is through occupying (having power over?) certain institutions that the powerful realize their will: "It is over these institutional means of power that the truly powerful are, in the first instance, powerful."[13] These institutions, "the strategic command posts of the social structure," are "the big corporations," "the machinery of the state," and "the military establishment."[14] "These hierarchies of state and corporation and army constitute the means of power; as such they are now of a consequence not before equaled in human history—and at their summits, there are now those command posts of modern society which offer us the sociological key to an understanding of the role of the higher circles in America."[15]

Now why is not religion, the Church, a major institution in present-day society? Why are the universities not major institutions of power? It is, presumably, because the big decisions are not made there; "the symbols of all these lesser institutions are used to legitimate the power and the decisions of the big three."[16] The big decisions are made in the big institutions, and the big institutions are those in which the big decisions are made. Not to put too fine a point on it, there is a vicious circle here, which points to a fundamental flaw in Mills' conception of social and historical reality. Is it, then, Mills' thesis that in these institutions occupied by the power elite, the decisions are made that . . . shape history?, determine the shape of society? Not exactly. "In so far as national events are decided, the power elite are those who decide them."[17] But are national events in fact "decided?" In *The Rise of American Civilization* (1942), narrated by Charles and Mary Beard, historians of some influence on Mills, how much was "decided"? Indeed, writes Mills:

It is not my thesis that for all epochs of human history and in all nations, a creative minority, a ruling class, an omnipotent elite, shape all historical events. Such statements, upon careful examination, usually turn out to be mere tautologies, and even when they are not, they are so entirely general as to be useless in the attempt to understand the history of the present. The minimum definition of the power elite as those who decide whatever is decided of major consequence, does not imply that the members of this elite are always and necessarily the history-makers; neither does it imply that they never are. We must not confuse the conception of the elite, which we wish to define, with one theory about their role: that they are the history-makers of our time.[18]

So the power elite are not the history-makers of our time. Nor are they the decision-makers, precisely; for we cannot give a precise account even of decision-making. "The idea of the power elite implies nothing about the process of decision-making as such; it is an attempt to delimit the social areas within which that process, whatever its character, goes on. It is a conception of who is involved in the process.[19]

And yet there are "pivotal moments," Mills writes. "[I]n our time the pivotal moment does arise," "and at that moment, small circles do decide or fail to decide."[20] And Mills lists five such moments in recent history: the dropping of the A-bomb on Japan, the decision on Korea, the "confusion" about Quemoy and Matsu, the "confusion" about Dien Bien Phu, and the "sequence of maneuvers" which involved the United States in World War II. "Is it not true that much of the history of our times is composed of such moments? And is not that what is meant when it is said that we live in a time of big decisions, of decisively centralized power?"[21]

Now all these pivotal moments, which we may agree are pivotal moments, involve warfare. And military history, narrowly defined, may indeed be made up of such moments. The die is cast; Caesar crosses the Rubicon. And yet Mills himself, as we shall see, emphatically rejects the "military metaphysic," the definition of reality in military terms. But let us consider one of these moments, the decision not to intervene militarily in the colonial war in Indochina in 1954. As reported by Fox Butterfield, in *The Pentagon Papers, as published by the New York Times* (not available, of course, to Mills):

> The Government's internal record shows, . . . that while Secretary of State John Foster Dulles and Adm. Arthur W. Radford, Chairman of the Joint Chiefs of Staff, pushed hard for intervention, other service chiefs, particularly Gen. Matthew B. Ridgeway of the Army, were more cautious. They remembered the bitter and protracted experience in Korea and were not eager to repeat it.
> President Eisenhower finally reached a decision against intervention on April 4 after a meeting of Dr. Dulles and Admiral Radford with Congressional leaders the previous day showed that the Congress would not support American action without Allied help.[22]

(One of the considerations of Eisenhower at that time was that "The United States will not agree to a 'white man's party' to determine the problems of the Southeast Asian nations."[23] And yet the United States did "decide" to intervene, although not with military assistance at Dien Bien Phu; and indeed, the National Security Council had "decided," in 1952, "to prevent the countries of Southeast Asia from passing into the Communist orbit, and to assist them to develop will and ability to resist communism from within and without [also, presumably, by "decision"] and to contribute to the strengthening of the free world."[24] The subsequent history of the struggle in Indochina is the well-known succession of "decisions": to establish a client regime in South Vietnam; to ignore the Geneva accords; to introduce American military personnel; to escalate; to bomb; to spread the war to Laos and Cambodia, etc., etc.

In all these decisions, the power elite failed to realize its will, its objective of defeating the national, communist, anti-imperialist movement in Southeast Asia. From this we may draw either of two conclusions: (1) that the power elite simply was not powerful enough, in the sense that a witch-doctor may not have enough magic, i.e., that it did not have enough planes, enough bombs, etc., which throughout the war has been the premise of the power elite itself; or (2) that history is not decided by power elites, is not *willed* by individuals or cliques, just as nature is not willed by witch-doctors. (The parallel between nature and history is not inexact; for as Marx writes, "History itself is . . . nature's coming to be man.")[25]

This is the sense of "the struggle against history," about which N. D. Houghton and others have written: the impotence of power elites in the face of deep-rooted historical trends. But surely, we may think, the struggle itself is willed and decided. To a degree, this may be true; reaction is willed if anything in history is willed. In a deeper sense, however, anti-anti-imperialism is willed no more than anti-imperialism: the reactionary struggles no more than the progressive, as the history of Indochina, subsequent to the American decision *not* to intervene, has indicated. As the leading power of the capitalist world, the United States was drawn irresistibly into the Indochinese struggle. Or perhaps, we should say, in Marxist terms, the American "ruling class" was so drawn. But as Richard Rovere observes, commenting on Mills:

Marx's "classes" do not "decide" or plot or plan or do anything, but behave as the pressures of history compel them to behave. It has been interesting to note that when Mills, some years after writing *The Power Elite*, became enthusiastic about Fidel Castro's Cuba, he tended to lapse into traditional Marxism. He saw not "interlocking directorates" or "overlapping cliques" bring Castro to power or maintain him there. He described the Cuban revolution not as a plot but as a movement of restless, surging humanity struggling to fulfill its needs and aspirations.[26]

When Marx writes that "History is nothing but men realizing their aims," it is to that "movement of restless, surging humanity" that he is referring. Thus the alternative to the theory of the power elite is not, as Mills believes, "history as fate," "impersonal drift." It is a theory, indeed, of man as the subject and not the object of history; for both Marx and Mills agree that "history does not go on behind men's backs"; but of man not as *will*, which as we see, ends up in an obscurantist elitism, but as *need;* nature coming to be man, precisely.

It is more precisely, a theory of history unfolding in accordance with the productive powers expressive of the needs of social classes, and ultimately, providentially, perhaps, of the needs of a society which divides itself into social classes; a theory of history, in Marx's conception, which postulates, as the end of history—or otherwise, the end of "pre-history"—the ascendance of the universal class, the proletariat, that vast body of need; humanity, once again, undivided.

It was the need of the bourgeoisie, embodying a new *praxis*, new needs and new ways of satisfying need, that produced, through the struggles of many generations, the bourgeois revolution. It is the need of the proletariat, the universal class—whether or not that be the industrial working class, as Marx knew it, need not concern us now—that will, through "new forms of intercourse," transform the very essence of need, by transforming labor, which satisfies need, into "self-activity." It is also the need of the proletariat which will as in Mills' collective dream of the Left, subject the conditions of life, in nature and society, to the greatest degree possible, to the power of individuals.

These various conditions, which appear first as conditions of self-activity, later as fetters upon it, form in the whole evolution of history a coherent series of forms of intercourse, the coherence of which consists in this: that in the place of an earlier form of intercourse, which has become a fetter, a new one is put, corresponding to the more developed productive forces and, hence to the advanced mode of the self-activity of individuals—a form which in its turn becomes a fetter and is then replaced by another. Since these conditions correspond at every stage to the simultaneous development of the productive forces, their history is at the same time the history of the evolving productive forces taken over by each new generation, and is therefore the history of the development of the forces of the individuals themselves.[27] . . . Thus, while the refugee serfs only wished to be free to develop and assert those conditions of existence which were already there, and hence, in the end, only arrived at free labor, the proletarians, if they are to assert themselves as individuals, will have to abolish the very condition of their existence hitherto (which has, moreover, been that of all society up to the present), namely, labor.[28]

Thus we see how fateful it is, theoretically and practically, to amend Marx's theory of classes and of the role of class struggle in history, as Mills has done in *The Power Elite*; to amend, following Weber, the theory of "economic determinism," which as we have seen, is in essence a theory about material need, "the actual life-process," as Marx so often writes. We see, schematically, and shall later see in greater detail, how fateful is the substitution of the term "power elite" for Marx's "ruling class." Mills writes:

The simple Marxian view makes the big economic man the real holder of power; the simple liberal view makes the big political man the chief of the power system; and there are some who would view the warlords as virtual dictators. Each of these is an over simplified view. It is to avoid them that we use the term "power elite" rather than, for example, "ruling class."

And in a note:

> It should be clear to the reader by now that we do not accept as adequate the simple view that high economic men unilaterally make all decisions of national consequence. We hold that such a simple view of "economic determinism" must be elaborated by "political determinism" and "military determinism"; that the higher agents of each of these three domains now often have a noticeable degree of autonomy; and that only in the often intricate ways of coalition do they make up and carry through the most important decisions. [29]

Now as Herbert Aptheker remarks, "Marxism, in its emphasis on the 'economic,' is not referring to the 'big economic man'; it is referring to the property relationships characterizing the social order and is insisting that upon that base is reared, with interpenetration, the rest of the juridical, political, ideological, and cultural features of the society." [30] More simply, Marxism is referring to economic need, material need,—animal need, if you will—as the motor force, the "motive power," as we will remember, which Mills denies in his early theory that "motives are words," in social and cultural development. The theory of the ruling class is as much a theory of natural history as it is of history. Thus Marx writes:

> All history is the preparation for "man" to become the object of sensuous consciousness, and for the needs of "man as man" to become (natural, sensuous) needs. History itself is a real part of natural history—of nature's coming to be man. Natural science will in time subsume under itself the science of man, just as the science of man will subsume under itself natural science. [31]

It is as part of this process that ruling classes rise and fall; and the decline of ruling classes, their ultimate demise, their disappearance in history, is as important a part of their history as their ascendency. This *history* of ruling classes, this problem as T.B. Bottomore writes, of "how to explain the rise and fall of ruling elites," [32] is largely evaded by Mills.

Indeed, nothing that *develops* in nature or culture—no painting, book, or civilization—develops primarily through the decisions of isolated consciousness. And it is decidedly not the case that what is not subject to conscious decision develops, as Mills writes, as "fate," "blind drift." Rather, germinating, exfoliating—like onions in the dark cupboard, like the book in the author's secret mind, like the secret workings, the secret wisdom, of the body—it is the highest embodiment of purpose. And this is indeed the conscious lesson of the social struggles of the 1960's, here and abroad, above all in France, May, 1968. As Rosa Luxemburg, a "revolutionary to the core," as Mills acknowledges, wrote:

The unconscious comes before the conscious. The logic of the historic process comes before the subjective logic of the human beings who participate in the historic process. The tendency is for the directing organs of the socialist party to play a conservative role. Experience shows that every time the labor movement wins new terrain those organs work it to the utmost. They transform it at the same time into a kind of bastion, which holds up advance on a wider scale. [33]

And for this we have the testimony also of Trotsky in exile, the Trotsky who actually helped make a revolution, and build a revolutionary society (perhaps wiser in exile than he was in power):

The organic character of social processes, including political ones, is revealed with a special immediacy during critical epochs, when the old "revolution-ary" organizations are shown to possess hindquarters of lead, which prevent them from performing the necessary about-face at the right moment. . . . The social processes, in the broad sense, are much closer to organic than to mechanical ones. A revolutionary who relies on the scientific theory of social development is much closer in his mode of thinking and working to the doctor, . . . than to the engineer. . . . Like the doctor, the revolutionary Marxist has to rely on the autonomous rhythm of the vital processes. . . . But it must be a question of participation in an *organic* process. One must know its laws, as a doctor must know the "healing power of nature." [34]

This question of the conscious and the unconscious in history—of what is willed and decided, and what is spontaneous—is of crucial importance at this juncture. It is the question of elitism and populism, of democracy and oligarchy: the question, as Rosa Luxemburg wrote, of Leninism or Marxism. In the present context, if we may take liberalism as the political theory of bourgeois democ-racy, it is the question of liberalism or Marxism. It is the question of the power elite and of mass society. It is the question, with which Mills begins his career, of the theory of mind. (The translator of Durkheim's great work, *The Division of Labor in Society*, emphasizes that the key term of Durkheimian sociology, *conscience*, is closer to "unconsciousness" than to "consciousness," as it is customarily translated: ". . .the term has resemblance to the term 'unconscious' in psychoanalysis, rather than to consciousness in logical theory. The

terms 'collective' and 'commune' Durkheim employed interchange-
ably in referring to a conscience of such a sort.")[35]

Mills is indeed not unaware of his head-on collision with the point
of view represented by Rosa Luxemburg, the essence of whose life
and work, lies in "her belief," as Mills puts it, "in the revolutionary
spontaneity of the proletarian masses." And Mills continues:

She is in this respect a very close follower of the basic ideas of Karl Marx. His
ambiguity at this point is hers. On no point is this clearer than in her view that
democratic procedures and the socialist revolution *must* coincide. She had
one foot in The Second International, one foot in The Third, and her head, I
am afraid, in the cloudier, more utopian reaches of classic marxism.[36]

Now Luxemburg's emphasis on the spontaneity of the masses is not
cloudy and utopian. Quite the contrary, it is the theory of the power
elite, as we have been laboring to demonstrate, that is cloudy, and, if
you will, utopian. (It is the same theory which is the premise of *New
Men of Power*.) The spontaneity of the masses, a fact so glaring as to
blind us to it, is the underlying reality of history.

It is, of course, impossible to document this thesis here, much less
"prove" it: the thesis, as Georges LeFebvre has written, of "history
from below." Nor do LeFebvre, Rude, Soboul, Hobsbawn, and
others necessarily advance their view point as a general theory of
history (no more than does Mills his theory in *The Power Elite*). Yet it
is the thrust of this Marxist-oriented scholarship, and of a perennial
tradition in social thought, seen in Machiavelli, that the great arbiters
of history are the people, the laboring masses, who daily produce, in
its infinite detail, the life of society; that the shaping forces of history
come from the people, the many millions of farmers, traders,
artisans, intellectuals, and yes, rebels, adventurers, thieves, and
general riffraff, like the "wretched refuse" who settled America; that
history is made, in short, as the historian Michelet wrote late in the
last century, by *"le peuple tout entier,"* all the people. This is a theory
of history no more cloudy than that of the power elite; and indeed,
since power elites do not drop from heaven but also come "from
below," from the people, it is a theory that may claim a certain
necessary precedence. As Luxemburg writes:

Thus the colossal general strike in south Russia came into being in the
summer of 1903. By many small channels of partial economic struggles and
little "accidental" occurrences it flowed rapidly into a raging sea, and
changed the entire south of the Czarist empire for some weeks into a bizarre

revolutionary workers' republic. "Brotherly embraces, cries of delight and of enthusiasm, songs of freedom, merry laughter, humor and joy, were seen and heard in the crowd of many thousands of people which surged through the town from morning to evening. The mood was exalted; one could almost believe that a new, better life was beginning on the earth. A most solemn and at the same time an idyllic, moving spectacle." . . . So wrote at the time the correspondent of the Liberal *Ostoposhdonye* of Peter Struve.[37]

## WHO ARE THESE REVOLUTIONARIES?

The whole long scale runs from the regular trade-union struggle of a picked and tested troop of the proletariat drawn from large-scale industry, to the formless protest of a handful of rural proletarians, and to the first light stirrings of an agitated military garrison; from the well-educated and elegant revolt in cuffs and white collars in the counting house of a bank to the shy-bold murmurings of a clumsy meeting of dissatisfied policemen in a smoke-grimed, dark and dirty guardroom.[38]

## AND IS NOT THE OUTCOME OF ALL THIS MERE VIOLENCE?

The revolution, . . . is something other and something more than bloodshed. In contradiction to the police interpretation, which views the revolution exclusively from the standpoint of street disturbances and rioting, that is, from the standpoint of "disorder," the interpretation of scientific Socialism sees in the revolution above all a thorough-going internal reversal of social class relations.[39]

This "internal reversal of class relations," this deep organic process, with all its dark filamentary complexity, is the secret concealed in the theory of the power elite. "Who fathers the Power Elite?" is Mills' difficult question. His answer varies. Sometimes he seems to think that the power elite has no father, that it originates somehow outside or above society, or that it is self-originating and self-perpetuating—the theory, as George Jackson wrote, of "a society above society." Thus, says Mills, "The American elite entered modern history as a virtually unopposed bourgeoisie."[40] At other times the explanation is that the power elite *inherits* from its father; the question of inheritance, which as we saw earlier, is crucial in Mills' theory of socialism and of the distinction between socialism and capitalism: "The major economic fact about the very rich is the fact of the accumulation of advantages: those who have great wealth are in a dozen strategic positions to make it yield further wealth."[41]

These observations about wealth and power are, to be sure, empirically and theoretically cogent. And yet they conceal a distortion which fundamentally infects Mills' image of society. In an article of 1945, "The American Business Elite: A Collective Portrait," this distortion, this flaw in the lens of Mills' sociological imagination, is exposed with special sharpness. The article is a study, based on a survey of *The Dictionary of American Biography*, of the "historical elite of the United States," as consisting of people born between 1570 and 1879.

Mills divides the men studied into seven generations, the colonial; the pre-Revolutionary; the Revolutionary; the younger Revolutionary; the generation of the Napoleonic wars, born 1760-1789; the generation of the migrations beyond the Alleghanies, born 1790-1819; the Civil War generation and the post-Civil War generation, born 1850–1879. From his data he derives "the fact of the overwhelming upper-class production of upper-class businessmen. . . . The best statistical chance of becoming a member of the business elite is to be born into it."[42]

And yet, there is an anomaly in the data. "In each of the generations, except one, 1790–1819, business and the professions produced the majority of the business elite," Mills writes.[43] "This and the preceding and the following generations (comprising the total span 1760–1849), contain the modal proportions of the sons of farmers and skilled laborers. This span of years also contains the highest proportion of men of lower-class origin to enter the elite."[44] Moreover—and here we move closer to the later theory of the power elite—"Although eminent American business men have participated quite heavily in the political life of the United States," in the same generation there is a sharp drop in the proportion of business elite holding office. "This drop," writes Mills,"seems difficult to understand."[45]

The period of the anomalies which Mills finds difficult to understand is the period of the American Revolution. The drop in the proportion of businessmen holding public office and the rise in the proportion of businessmen who did not inherit from their fathers reflect nothing more than Luxemburg's "internal reversal of class relations," which occurs in times of social revolution—the tremors in the social bedrock, which rearrange, to a greater or lesser degree, the class structure of society. What is difficult to understand, from this point of view, is not the reversal of class relations as the generations succeed one another (a total, in Mills' study, of about twelve generations), but the perpetuation of class relations; not the revolutionary phases of social development, but the conservative ones.

What is difficult to understand, is how social change occurs at all if "the best statistical chance of becoming a member of the business elite is to be born into it" and if "the father of the business elite has typically been a business man."

And yet, Mills acknowledges, social change does go on, although not, as a rule, from below. There have, over the generations, been "changes in the American structure of power." And these changes "have generally come about by institutional shifts in the relative portions of the political, the economic, and the military orders."[46] But they have not, on the whole, involved "any ideological struggle to control masses." They have been changes in the makeup of the power elite.

In describing ongoing social change, Mills attempts, but largely fails to bring off, a historical view of the power elite. He fails perhaps because his point of view is so elitist. According to this description, "The American power elite has gone through four epochs, and now is well into a fifth."[47] The elite of the earliest period, the several decades following the Revolution, "are political men of education and of administrative experience, and, as Lord Bryce notes, 'possess a certain largeness of view and dignity of character.' " During the early nineteenth century, "the 'elite' became a plurality of top groups, each in turn quite loosely made up."[48] The post-Civil War period was marked by "the supremacy of corporate economic power"; the corporate economy "was the dynamic"; "the economic elite overshadowed the political."[49] The New Deal was a political decade, "essentially a balance of pressure groups and interest blocs." "For the first time in United States history, social legislation and lower-class issues became important features of the reform movement."[50]

This, the fifth epoch of the American power elite, is marked by "the decline of politics as genuine and public debate of alternative decisions"; by the "military ascendancy"; and by the creation of a "permanent war economy." "The warlords have gained decisive political relevance, and the military structure of America is now in considerable part a political structure."[51]

Of these historical *apercus*, it is perhaps the concept of the permanent war economy, the product of what Eisenhower, three years after the publication of Mills' book, dubbed "the military-industrial complex," that has the most analytical leverage. And yet it is by no means clear in Mills what the rationale of the permanent war economy is, and how it has come about. Have the militarists simply *imposed* this economy, and its attendant "metaphysics"? "The warlords, along with fellow travelers and spokesmen, are attempting to plant their metaphysics firmly among the population at large."[52]

There is, Mills tells us, a "great structural shift of modern American capitalism toward a permanent war economy."[53] But the historical reality underlying this shift is nowhere clearly stated. According to Marxism, this historical reality, to put it simply, is capitalism— structural economic shifts. The exigencies of monopoly capitalism, in its last stage of imperialism (which Mills never directly discusses in this volume), require the permanent war economy to fortify it against economic crisis at home and to maintain its empire, also an internal exigency, abroad. Either this kind of social analysis has become too plain and vulgar for Mills since he wrote on "behemoth" in 1942, or the specter of the power elite has crowded it out of his mind.

But there is, underlying the unexplained structural shift toward the power elite, a deeper-lying structural change, explicitly addressed by Mills. This is the shift toward a "mass society," largely a matter, Mills writes, of "impersonal drift." We have read about the top, the power elite.

But how about the bottom? As all these trends have become visible at the top and on the middle, what has been happening to the great American public? If the top is unprecedently powerful and increasingly unified and willful; if the middle zones are increasingly a semi-organized stalemate—in what shape is the bottom, in what condition is the country at large? The rise of the power elite, we shall now see, rests upon and in some ways is part of, the transformation of the publics of America into a mass society.[54]

With Mills' critique of mass society, we come round full circle to the social theory of mind, of language, of communication, of action, which so preoccupied him at the beginning of his career. In part this critique turns on a semantic shift, which reflects the "conservative mood" which Mills decries in the penultimate chapter of *The Power Elite*. Rosa Luxemburg, as we have seen, wrote of mass strikes and demonstrations; radicals of the 1920's spoke of the New Masses; Maoists of today affirm that history is made by the great masses. Mills, distinguishing between "publics," which are good, and "masses," which are bad, writes: "as publics become masses, masses sometimes become crowds; and, in crowds, the psychical rape by the mass media is supplemented up-close by the harsh and subtle harangue. Then the people in the crowd disperse again—as atomized and submissive masses."[55]

And publics, once again, the "classic public of democratic theory,"[56] the "classic bourgeois public,"[57] are rooted in the Jeffersonian "scatter of small producers:

What is happening might again be stated in terms of the historical parallel between the economic market and the public of public opinion. In brief, there is a movement from widely scattered little powers to concentrated powers and the attempt at monopoly control from powerful centers, which, being partially hidden, are centers of manipulation as well as of authority. The small shop serving the neighborhood is replaced by the anonymity of the national corporation: mass advertisement replaces the personal influence of opinion between merchant and customer. The political leader hooks up his speech to a national network and speaks, with appropriate personal touches, to a million people he never saw and never will see. Entire brackets of professions and industries are in the "opinion business," impersonally manipulating the public for hire.[58]

Now we might suppose, following Marx, that as economic life is progressively socialized, as the scatter of small producers is succeeded by associated production, as people enter into more manifold relationships with one another, as the means of communication grow more complex and sophisticated, democracy becomes a greater and deeper reality. But this *a priori* supposition does indeed seem to be refuted by our present mass society, which is not one of broadened horizons, but as Mills writes, "narrow milieux." The painful truth about the American people does indeed seem to be this:

Sunk in their routines, they do not transcend, even by discussion, much less by action, their more or less narrow lives. They do not gain a view of the structure of their society and of their role as a public within it. The city is a structure composed of such little environments and the people in them tend to be detached from one another. The "stimulating variety" of the city does not stimulate the men and women of the "bedroom belt," the one-class suburbs, who can go through life knowing only their own kind. If they do reach for one another, they do so only through stereotypes and prejudiced images of the creatures of other milieux. Each is trapped by his confining circle; each is cut off from easily identifiable groups. It is for people in such narrow milieux that the mass media can create a pseudo-world beyond, and a pseudo-world within themselves as well.[59]

Thus the flight to the suburbs of the middle-aged, which does indeed seem to be part of a national policy, ensconcing masses of people in "narrow milieux"; and, more hopefully, the flight from the suburbs of the young. What has gone wrong? An easy answer is the Marxist one: the "forces of production" have been *de facto* socialized; the "relations of production," the relations of the producers to these forces, and to each other—the mode of cooperation being both a relation of production and a force of production—remain private.

Since the "privatized man," as we recall from Mills himself, is an idiot, and America is a nation of privatized men, this situation may be described as Marx's "idiocy of rural life" raised to the highest suburbanized degree. This is a society of tremendously socialized production, whose social relations remain precisely those of the Jeffersonian scatter.

We have from Marx the leading premise: modern industrial society. But we are missing the middle term: industrial democracy, social democracy, labor democracy; in a word, socialism. This is the middle term on which Mills staked his hopes in his book on labor, and which he has now dispaired of, or perhaps, in the dismal 1950's, simply forgotten. And thus we have as our conclusion, in the orthography of the New Left . . . Amerika.

But Mills has not simply forgotten about labor democracy. He has, as we have seen, an ambiguous attitude toward it from the beginning. It is thus that he writes:

The idea of a mass society suggests the idea of an elite of power. The idea of the public, in contrast, suggests the liberal tradition of a society without any power elite, or at any rate with shifting elites of no sovereign consequence. For, if a genuine public is sovereign, it needs no master; but the masses, in their full development, are sovereign only in some plebiscitarian moment of adulation to an elite as authoritative celebrity. The political structure of a democratic state requires the public; and, the democratic man, in his rhetoric, must assert that this public is the very seat of sovereignty.[60]

Mills struggled toward a social theory of mind but ended only with the isolated thinker; he extolled ancient China, whose language was an emblem of collective life, but formulated a theory of language as social control; he pragmatistically yearned to break out into action, from the Cartesian circle of doubt and belief, but clung to the inhibitions of his behaviorist theory of motives. It is indeed true that for Mills, "the idea of a mass society suggests the idea of an elite of power." This is the dilemma of a late bourgeois thinker, caught in the middle, in search of community and in flight from community.

And what of the society of "publics" and their "opinions"? (A notion which Mills perhaps derives from Walter Lippmann) Mills writes thus:

The people are presented with problems. They discuss them. They decide on them. They formulate viewpoints. These viewpoints are organized, and they compete. One viewpoint "wins out." Then the people act out this view, or their representatives are instructed to act it out, and this they promptly do.[61]

There is something strangely lifeless, bloodless, stultifying, or perhaps better still, simply *unreal*, in this conception of politics; surely something has been left out. The ultimate trivialization, the reduction to absurdity of this view of the democratic process is the opinion poll, by which the will of the people is registered, and presidents chart their policies thereby—a specialty, to be sure, of a kind of sociology that Mills despised. As Karl Mannheim comments:

The development of this approach to political problems was an historical and lasting achievement of the bourgeoisie, and its value may be appreciated even when the onesidedness of its intellectualism has been completely laid bare. The bourgeois mind had a vital social interest in concealing from itself, by means of this intellectualism, the limits of its own rationalization. Hence it acted as if real conflicts could be fully settled by discussion. It did not realize, however, that closely connected with the realm of politics there arose a new kind of thinking in which theory could not be separated from practice nor thought from intent.

For here it becomes once more apparent that socialist thought begins at that point where bourgeois democratic thought reaches its limits, and that it threw new light on just those phenomena which its predecessors, because of the intimate connection with their own interests, had left in the dark. To Marxism belongs the credit for discovering that politics does not consist merely in parliamentary parties and the discussions they carry on, and that these, in whatever concrete form they appear, are only surface expressions of deeper-lying economic and social situations which can be made intelligible to a large extent through a new mode of thought. These discoveries signalize the raising of the discussion to a higher level from which a more inclusive view of history and a clearer conception of what actually constitutes the domain of politics can be obtained.[62]

And Mills does indeed go on to say, that whereas "in the democratic society of publics it was assumed that among the individuals who composed it there was a natural and peaceful harmony of interests . . . this essentially conservative doctrine gave way to the Utilitarian doctrine that such a harmony of interests had first to be created by reform before it could work, and later to the Marxian doctrine of class struggle, which surely was then, and certainly is now, closer to reality than any assumed harmony of interests."[63]

Now perhaps we are getting closer to a living politics. To the "intellectual" conception, as Mills says, of politics as discussion—but it is a trivial conception even of intellect—we should add an affectional and conative dimension. Our conception of politics surely should embrace passion (as Weber, indeed, insisted). And as we saw in our chapter on the white collar people, what principally afflicts them and immobilizes them, so that they do not move to change their circumstances, to shake up their narrow milieux—in a word, to act—is that they do not *feel*. Intrinsic to the "discussion process," and not supervening on it, not ancillary to it, must be, as Mills writes, the "opportunity for people to act out their opinions collectively," an opportunity which as Mills adds, "is of course limited by their position in the structure of power."

Now indeed we are closer to Machiavelli, to Rosa Luxemburg, and indeed, to the Marxism of Mao Tse-tung, who also calls for *speech* in the working out of social "contradictions":

. . . some comrades are afraid of the masses, their criticism, and what they say. Are there any grounds on which a Marxist-Leninist can justify this fear? If he does not talk about his own mistakes or allow others to talk about them, the fear will grow. I do not think a fear of this kind is necessary. What is there to be afraid of? Our attitude is to hold fast to truth and correct our mistakes. The questions of right or wrong, correct or mistaken, belong to the category of the internal contradictions of the people which can be resolved only by the method of reasoning, discussing, criticism and self-criticism. In short, by democratic methods, by allowing the masses to speak up. [64] . . . Letting other people speak will not lead to the sky falling down on us nor to one's own downfall. What will happen if we do not allow others to speak? In that case one day we ourselves will inevitably fall. [65]

Politics must follow the mass line. It will not do to rely on leaders alone. How can the leaders do so much? The leaders can cope with only a fraction of everything, good and bad. Consequently, everybody must be mobilized to share the responsibility, to speak up, to encourage other people, and to criticize other people. Everyone has a pair of eyes and a mouth and he must be allowed to see and speak up. Democracy means allowing the masses to manage their own affairs. Here are two ways: one is to depend on a few individuals and the other is to mobilize the masses to manage affairs. Our politics is mass politics. [66]

Now how do we "mobilize the masses"? Or better, if the initiative is to come from the masses, how do they get themselves mobilized? Here is the role of what Mills calls "voluntary organizations," "the citizen's major link with decision":[67] "assemblages and political rallies, parliamentary sessions, law-court debates, small discussion circles dominated by one man, open discussion circles with talk moving freely back and forth among fifty people, and so on."[68]

But here again, the conception is abstract, lifeless. What are these voluntary organizations, and on what basis are they organized? Political debate must be rooted in real, subpolitical circumstances, political consciousness must be rooted in everyday life. (Consciousness, as Marx writes, can only be "conscious existence," and once again, "existence determines consciousness.") These organizations, if they are to be relevant and real, must be organizations not of merely formal, political, abstract democracy, but as Mills saw clearly in his book on labor, social, work democracy. They must be organized in factories, offices, shops, schools, and in a multitude of milieux which only social democracy will bring into being. Like many others, from Thomas Paine to Marc Chagall, in the midst of revolutionary upheaval, which always engenders a multitude of new types of association, indeed, is the production of new types of association, Mao is able to write:

Many new things have begun to emerge in the great proletarian Cultural Revolution. The cultural revolutionary groups, committees, and other organizational forms created by the masses in many schools and units are something new and of great historical importance.

These cultural revolutionary groups, committees and congresses are excellent new forms of organization whereby under the leadership of the Communist Party the masses are educating themselves. They are an excellent bridge to keep our party in close contact with the masses. They are organs of power of the proletarian Cultural Revolution.

The struggle of the proletariat against the old ideas, culture, customs and habits left over from all the exploiting classes over thousands of years will necessarily take a very, very long time. Therefore, the cultural revolutionary groups, committees and congresses should not be temporary organizations but permanent, standing mass organizations. They are suitable not only for colleges, schools and government and other organizations, but generally also for factories, mines, other enterprises, urban districts and villages.

It is necessary to institute a system of general elections, like that of the Paris Commune, for electing members to the cultural revolutionary groups and committees and delegates to the cultural revolutionary congresses. The lists of candidates should be put forward by the revolutionary masses after full discussion, and the elections should be held after the masses have discussed the lists over and over again.[69]

"Are they free, are they happy?" This is perhaps the most important question about the power elite. In the opinion of Mills, who as an independent Leftist, early espoused the "wish that man should be enthusiastic and joyous," the answer is "Yes, within the terms of their society, they are really free. . . . Money provides power and power provides freedom." As for happiness, "if the rich are not happy, it is because none of us are happy. . . . We simply must believe that the American rich are happy, else our confidence in the whole endeavor might be shaken."[70]

Once again, the question turns on an understanding of power. "Whatever else it may mean," Mills writes, "freedom means that you have the power to do what you want to do, when you want to do it, and how you want to do it."[71] Let us assume that freedom means what Mills says it means. (We shall overlook the fact that Mills says both that *power* gives you the *freedom* to do what you want and that *freedom* gives you the *power* to do what you want, suggesting that Mills is less interested here in rigorous thought, than in expressing a certain sour attitude.) Whether money gives you the power to do what you want, and hence the power to exercise your freedom, depends on what you want to do. Suppose that you want to write a book, or be a musical person, or an accomplished athlete. Money will not give you the power to do any of these things, although it may buy you literacy, leisure, teachers, equipment of all sorts, etc. In all those things that involve real human powers, money is of no avail, except in so far as socially, in cooperation with a multitude of factors over which individuals are largely powerless, it makes possible a certain level of culture and opportunity.

This is not to deny that having money is greatly advantageous in class society—which is not Mills' point precisely—nor that "wealth in America is directly gratifying and directly leads to many further gratifications."[72] But those *powers*, those "whims and fantasies," as Mills writes, which money directly realizes—and it is, once again, a question of the *power* which money provides, to *freely* do what you want to do—are not, on the whole, essential human powers; and their exercise, however trite it may seem to emphasize this, does not essentially gratify. Money may buy you a record collection, but it cannot give you the power to enjoy music. Indeed, as Marx wrote, it may, through the dynamic of private property, the "sense of *having*," alienate you from your native musicality. It may buy you a tour of the world, but it cannot make you a good traveler; it may, because it confers on you an alienated power, the power not to *enjoy*, as we may say, but to *possess*, make you an alienated and a bad traveler.

This is to say that those gratifications which money provides, according to its own power, are not, as Marx writes, specific expressions of your real individual life—not gratifications of your own nature; and at the same time, that they are not *species*-gratifications, not essentially *human*. Mills, like Marx, has a self-realization, or as he writes, self-cultivation, theory of freedom. But unlike Marx, he has no theory of the human, no theory of man. Or perhaps better, he has such a theory; he has a positive image of man and would wish men to be enthusiastic and joyous, but most of the time he despairs of it.

Because Mills has no theory of man, he cannot, as Plato wrote, distinguish between true and false pleasures, between real gratifications and false, illusory ones. (But everyone whom money [bourgeois society] has not rendered completely senseless can make this distinction without a theory.) Because he has no theory of man, he fails on the whole to see that true self-realization, true freedom, is a collective attribute, a species-attribute. For as Marx writes, "Only in community with others, has each individual the means of cultivating his gifts in all directions; only in the community, therefore, is personal freedom possible."[73]

It is thus that Mills can claim that the power elite are *free* but perhaps not *happy*! For in a real self-realization theory of freedom, freedom and happiness necessarily coincide. (This is clear, for example, in Spinoza.) But if freedom is a collective attribute, found only in community with others, then indeed, "If the rich are not happy it is because none of us are happy."[74] For is this not, as Mills has emphasized, a nation of idiots, of privatized men? How *could* we be happy?

Now this is not an article of faith, but empirically and logically verified. Ultimately, however, as at the start of our study, we come back to a question of belief:

. . . [T]o believe that [the rich] are unhappy would probably be un-American. For if they are not happy, then the very terms of success in America, the very aspirations of all sound men, lead to ashes rather than fruit.
Even if everyone in America, being human, were miserable, that would not be reason to believe that the rich were *more* miserable. And if everyone is happy, surely that is no reason to believe that the rich are excluded from the general bliss.[75]

Surely Mills is not going to join the chorus of American celebration which Norman Mailer, with Mills' own stamp freshly on him, so roundly denounced at the beginning of our chapter. Surely he is not going to join in the belief that everyone is happy in the suburbs, or would be happy in the suburbs, and that everything is basically all right. And not, presumably, because he is afraid of being un-American. Rather, because it would refute his life's work, and his most fundamental beliefs. And surely he is not going to fall into that other trap, the conservative trap, the belief that misery is human nature. And yet in a series of astonishing propositions, only half ironic, he is prepared to do just this. This confusion of values, this deflation of any sustaining belief in man, is the most dismal feature of the peaceful 1950's.

CHAPTER 6

# Listen Yankee! *Listen Sociologist!*

THE penultimate phase of Mills' career, before the head-on confrontation with Marx, comprehends three books published in rapid succession, but quite diverse in nature: *The Causes of World War Three* (1958), a re-statement, in a mood of heightened urgency, of earlier themes; *The Sociological Imagination* (1959), a reflective pause and summing-up, a genuine wisdom book; and looking toward the future, anxiously, hopefully, throwing a life-line over that wall that had always separated Mills from "history-making," the remarkable book on the Cuban Revolution, *Listen Yankee* (1961). (A fourth book, *Images of Man*, which we shall consider later, was published in 1961). Here, at last, there surges up the long suppressed, violent passion for social justice, rough frontier gun-on-the-hip justice, a passion which must have gripped the young Mills in the early years in Texas.

With the book on the power elite, Mills had reached an impasse. His "trilogy," on labor, the middle classes, and the upper classes (which he did not consent, as we will recall, to call in Marxist fashion the "ruling classes"), was complete. And in that airless room at the top, which included both his subject matter and his popular success, Mills began to gasp for air. We have already remarked that the thesis of the power elite is in part a Cold War fantasy. Now, with Mills' health faltering—he suffered his first heart attack in 1958 and was badly frightened—a reciprocal movement takes place, in both history and biography, as Mills would say, both objectively and subjectively, and the Cold War becomes a power elite fantasy.

Mills often addresses himself to various "definitions of reality." The Cold War is an elitist definition of reality; it is "the military metaphysic." The apogee of the elitist mentality, as Mills writes in

"Causes," is "the total war of absolute weapons." It is that brilliant
distillation of Cold War elitism, Dr. Strangelove. And Mills at this
point, as during World War II, we will recall, adopts the tone of a
certain Christian pacifism. As he writes in his "Pagan Sermon" to the
clergy: "Pacifism, we believe, is the test of your Christianity—and of
you."[1]

The types of social science, "types of reflection," as Mills writes,
are also definitions of reality, serving—and here we should glance
back at Mills' own early behaviorism—either human liberation, or, as
"Abstracted Empiricism" and "Grand Theory," serving "stable forms
of domination; the bureaucratic ethos," "illiberal practicality," "human engineering," "social control."[2]

Finally, "Revolution is a way of defining reality." "We revolutionaries," says Mills' Cuban to Mills' Yankee, "in our very
persons embody the anti-bureaucratic principle."[3] It is indeed, as
Andre Breton, also a revolutionary, wrote, a "surreal" definition of
reality—a fantasy, to be sure, but creative, expansive, and enliven-
ing!

Everyone has daydreams, but for most people these dreams are never related
to their everyday life. By our revolution, we Cubans have made The Big
Connection, between fantasy and reality, and now we are living in it. To us,
to live in this connection, that is the fact of our revolution.[4]

And what is the difference between this definition of reality and the
others, what is its guarantee of truth? Pragmatically, as Mills learned
long before, it is its meaning for life:

The revolution is a way of defining reality.
The revolution is a way of changing reality—and so of changing the
definitions of it.
The revolution is a moment of truth.[5]

And indeed, in this reality, defined by revolution, discovered or
re-discovered by Mills one year before his death, in this "Revolutionary Euphoria"—which Rosa Luxemburg so emphasized—Mills
once again finds breathing space and is moved to lay the power elite
theory finally to rest:

One of the many ways you are *not* helping us [says Mills' Cuban to Mills'
Yankee] is the curious idea you seem to have of how history is being made.
You always seem to think that those tens of thousands of people who are rising

up against you (eight million people, we have read, took part in the demonstrations against you in Japan recently), that they are just somehow misguided—and absolutely controlled by small conspiratorial groups of trouble makers, under direct orders from Moscow and Peking. You must think that they are diabolically omnipotent if you think that it is *they* who *create* all this messy unrest for you. . . . [6]

The "sociological imagination," as Mills writes time and time again, is imagination for "the intersections of history and biography":

The sociological imagination enables its possessor to understand the larger historical scene in terms of its meaning for the inner life and the external career of a variety of individuals. It enables him to take into account how individuals, in the welter of their daily experience, often become falsely conscious of their social positions. Within that shelter, the framework of modern society is sought, and within that framework the psychologies of a variety of men and women are formulated. By such means the personal uneasiness of individuals is focused upon explicit troubles and the indifference of publics is transformed into involvement with public issues. [7]

Historically, as we have said, these years of the 1950's were years of mixed complacency, anti-communism, nuclear terror. They were years, at Columbia University, where Mills was now a famous and beleaguered professor, of "no time for politics." They were years of fall-out and fallout shelters, when affluent homeowners, encouraged by such power elitists as Governor Rockefeller of New York, dug bunkers for themselves in their backyards, supplied with expensive survival goods from Hammacher Schlemmer; and it was debated, by theologians among others, whether such a family, secured against the end of the world, would have the right to drive less fortunate souls away from their door with machine gun fire. They were years of ultimate privatism, truly idiot years.

Biographically, these were years of crisis for Mills. In part this was the crisis of middle age in a hard-driving man who had made it—*The Power Elite* was a highly publicized best-seller. He was caught in the squeeze between popular success, sociological professionalism, and moral and political commitment; he did not know where to go from there. One symptom of this middle-of-the-journey crisis—in a journey which was to end abruptly, when the next turn in the road had barely come into sight—was a great deal of traveling and much contact with people in distant places. A tour of Eastern Europe in 1957–58 eventuated in a new view of the communist world, in great measure an admiring one, and one which involved Mills in some acrimonious controversy at home.

By 1960, as the new decade began, Kennedy was in the White House; America was plunged deep into the agonies and ecstasies of the civil rights movement; Castro had made it in Cuba; and the nationalist liberation movement had resumed in Asia. It was then, in the summer of 1960, that Mills visited Cuba; and it was in the fall of 1960 that he addressed his famous "Letter To The New Left."

It is difficult to say who had the greater influence: Mills on the New Left, or the New Left on Mills. Although his death, wrote Saul Landau, was for the young radicals, "the death of a prophet," Mills had not prophesized the young radicals—nor had anyone else, for that matter—and the vision of The People, Yes! which flickered in his book on labor was scarcely an ember. Indeed, in this very "Letter to the New Left," he reaffirms his "conception of the shape of power, the theory of the power elite," and denigrates "the labor metaphysic," the view of the laboring masses, or as the historian John Lukacs, quoted above, writes, "the inchoate movements of peoples" as the agency of historical change. He now favors another view, which we may call the mind metaphysic, according to which the "new generations of intellectuals around the world  [are] the real live agencies of historical change."[8] (Indeed, as Marx remarked, and as we shall have occasion to elaborate in our final chapter, "It is not enough that thought should seek its actualization; actuality must itself strive toward thought.")[9]

Nevertheless, Mills concludes his Letter, although not too clearly, not too sure of pitch, on a note which will sound loudly in *Listen, Yankee*. Urging his readers that their hopes are not utopian, Mills writes: "Whatever else it may be, it's not that. Tell it to the students of Japan. Tell it to the Negro sit-ins. Tell it to the Cuban Revolutionaries. Tell it to the people of the hungry-nation bloc."[10]

In the meantime, in a not unrelated polemic, Mills was settling old scores with establishment (power elite?) social science. Here again the key motif, sounded at the very outset of the work, is that of the relation between biography and history, "personal troubles" and "the public issues of social structure." Also sounded, perhaps more clearly than ever before, is a certain redemptive note, harkening back to Mills' early religiosity (which as we have seen continues to exert an influence throughout his life). As with "thoughts" and "motives," so with "personal troubles"; the thing is to transcend the privatistic trap—"Nowadays men often feel that their private lives are a series of traps," reads the first sentence in the book—and fight the problem out in the sphere of social, public, reality; in the social whole, the Durkheimian *collective;* in the sphere, pragmatistically and socialistically, of social transformation. Thus the sociological imagination is redemptive imagination; or in secular terms, as Mills' activities at the William Allison White Institute suggest, therapeutic imagination. (In this Mills is related to another, more hermetic figure—in most respects, quite dissimilar—enmeshed in the troubles of bourgeois decline, the philosopher Ludwig Wittgenstein.)

There are no private, individualistic, solutions, to the problems of intellectuals, white collar people, women, blacks, etc. Above all, a hard lesson, which Mills struggled with and against all his life, careerism, William James' Bitch Goddess Success, is not a solution. There are "facts of contemporary history" which transcend the anxiety-fraught "success and failure of individual men and women." And especially, perhaps, in a struggle, looming large today, which had a special poignancy for Mills, as his observations in *White Collar* suggest, of women. There is no private solution, indeed, no solution short of radical social transformation, to the agonizing problems of women in this society. And, as radical feminists are now teaching us, there is no solution to the problems of this society short of the radical transformation of the situation of women: "In so far as the family as an institution turns women into darling little slaves and men into their chief providers and unweaned dependents, the problem of a satisfactory marriage remains incapable of purely private solution."[11]

As Mills had learned from pragmatism, especially from Mead, the inner world of psychology and the outer world of action, individual and social, are ultimately indivisible. He had struggled, falsely, to articulate this in his early behaviorism and in his massive text on social psychology, *Character and Social Structure,* which he later judged to be "a lot of crap." "What they need"—what *we* need, troubled men and women—"and what they feel they need, is a quality of mind that will help them to use information and to develop reason in order to achieve lucid summations of what is going on in the world and of what may be happening within themselves. It is this quality, I am going to contend, that journalists and scholars, artists and public scientists and editors are coming to expect of what may be called the sociological imagination."[12]

Now as Mills again learned from pragmatism, Dewey in particular, it is in the sphere of *value* that problems, private and public, arise and are fought out: "To formulate issues and troubles, we must ask what values are cherished yet threatened, and what values are cherished and supported, by the characterizing trends of our period."[13] It is in the sphere of value that troubles are experienced and issues formulated. It is in the sphere of value that the sociological imagination arises and goes to work. This is Dewey's instrumental logic, the logic of the organism in the environment. Logic for Dewey is an intellectual function, but saturated with emotion and qualitative thought; as Dewey wrote, logic is an indivisible unity of fact and value—of the organism in the environment; but socialized, totalized, as sociological logic, sociological imagination—an *adaptational function*, it is clear, in Durkheimian-Marxist terms. It is, from Dewey's standpoint, Hegel naturalized, Darwinized; from Marx's standpoint, it is Darwin Hegelianized, socialized.

"The experience of indifference," impossible for the animal in the environment, but human, all too human, in the social environment, is thus throughout his life Mills' *bête noir*. It is because he realizes that the sphere of his sociological imagination is valuational, or more specifically, *sentient*, that Mills appeals so often to "sensibility" now and earlier. The appeal is most notable in *The Power Elite*—notwithstanding his persistent invocation of "reason." And it is for this reason, among others, that he now defines the task of sociology as "cultural," akin to literature: "It is my aim in this book to define the meaning of the social sciences for the cultural tasks of our time."[14] (We will recall Norman Mailer's angry remarks in the *Partisan Review* Symposium on "Our Culture.") From this point of view, we may regard the power elite theory as a *symptom*, akin to much anti-Semitism, anti-communism, anti-Romanism, etc., of this maladaptational "uneasiness and indifference." (Of course, the theory is rather anomalous in the context of the sociological imagination if it is understood as a theory that there is some controlling group responsible for our malaise, that must be exposed and held accountable, brought to justice.) It is a symptom, both individual and collective, subject to therapeutic analysis by Mills' own sociological imagination, of a maladaptation in the logic of the organism in the environment.

The signal fact about Mills' sociological imagination, as we already know, is that it does not sit well with conventional sociology; so much so that we may call it anti-sociology, and Mills the sociologist—the radical in the academy—the anti-sociologist. The conflict, and Mills' consquent isolation in academia, and his—also consequent—appeal to a new generation of antisociological sociologists, is as deep as that.

It is thus that Alvin W. Gouldner, very much under the influence of Mills, and a senior member of those critics of sociology from within, whose "prototype, . . . is C. Wright Mills," can write in 1970, in blanket terms, of the "Coming Crisis of Western Sociology." And although Gouldner includes Soviet Marxism in Western sociology and speaks of "the emerging crisis of Soviet Marxism,"[15] he sees as the hope of sociology, both as science and as "liberative potential" (if we may make that un-Marxist and probably un-Millsian distinction), its accelerating "convergence with Marxism," the living Marxism, presumably, which is not the ideology of Soviet bureaucracy, but the reality of the social process. Indeed, Gouldner writes, this is a dialectical development within academic sociology itself, within the ideology—"Functionalism" (more of this later)—of bourgeois social science: "In short, the analysis of social change is increasingly leading Functionalism toward a convergence with Marxism."[16]

In this, Gouldner's book of 1970 carries Mills' book of 1959 a giant step further—fully in keeping with the trend of the times. Indeed, it is difficult, from the present vantage point, to conceive of a social theory, in sociology, philosophy and history (for Marxism embraces all these fields, and it is only a certain parochialism which defines Marx principally as a sociologist) satisfying Mills' imagination, which is not essentially Marxist. And this is not merely a matter of intellectual history, that is, not merely academic. "Classical Marxism," writes Mills, when he is just beginning to shed the calloused skin of twenty years or more of disillusionment and Weberian pessimism, "has been central to the development of modern sociology; Max Weber, like so many other sociologists, developed much of his work in a dialogue with Karl Marx."[17] And again—and we look once more toward our final chapter—"So much of modern social science has been a frequently unacknowledged debate with the work of Marx, and a reflection as well of the challenge of socialist movements and communist parties."[18] Gouldner echoes him: "Indeed, much of the history of Academic Sociology during the Classical or third period is intelligible only as a response to and a polemic against Marxism."[19]

And yet, only a few years earlier, an erudite scholar, Henry Bamford Parkes, could publish a well-received book called *Marxism: An Autopsy* (and a prominent philosopher at Columbia in 1958 could pronounce to an aspiring undergraduate that "Social philosophy is dead"). Now it is of the greatest importance to emphasize that this is not simply a matter of intellectual fashion, and surely not of intellectual opinion-makers, intellectual power elites, working their elitist influence. If sociology is now tending toward a convergence with Marxism; if younger sociologists, political scientists, historians, philosophers, etc., are increasingly caught up in Marxism, as the academic insurgencies of recent years indicate; and if from our present vantage point the *past* bears so deeply, often unknowingly (Mills' "unacknowledged debate"), the stamp of Marx, this is because Marxism is not ideology, or is more than mere ideology, but the living *praxis* of our time—at least of our time. It is the truth of the social process. It is the living *praxis*, to quote once again the anti-communist Cold War historian John Lukacs, not of small intellectual circles, who have no independent *praxis*, contrary to one of Mills' deepest convictions, but of "the inchoate movements of peoples" (and of the ripening, fructifying movements of peoples, which bear their fruit, and go to seed and must inchoately begin again).[20]

The first of the bourgeois ideologies (although he does not expressly call them that) that Mills tackles is grand theory, whose leading representative is Talcott Parsons. And the first charge that Mills levels against Parsons, quoting lengthy specimens of his prose, is a literary one; "irrelevant ponderosity."[21] But Parsons' verbiage does indeed have meaning and social relevance, which Mills proceeds, to extract. There are, in all social thought, two key problems: social order and social change. Social order is Parsons' primary concern; he wants to defend it and he does so by elaborating a theory of "shared symbols, systems, and value orientations," making for "social equilibrium." As for social change, that is, history, as Mills writes, "This," in Mills' translation of Parsons, "I cannot explain very well, that is, in the terms of my Systematic and General Theory of the Social System."[22] As Mills sums it up, "The ideological meaning of grand theory tends strongly to legitimate stable forms of domination."[23] And, "given this social equilibrium, and all the socialization and control that man it, how is it possible that anyone should ever get out of line?"[24]

Now as we have seen, this is also a problem for Mills, the theorist of the power elite. It is, indeed, a problem for sociology in general, not only practically but theoretically. As in Epicurus, the atoms serve, but not merely by fiat. (Marx wrote his doctoral dissertation on "The Difference between the Democritean and Epicurean Philosophies of Nature"; he preferred the latter because in it the atom, which swerves, embodies freedom and an "energizing principle" for experience, arising from its nonindependence and its relation to other bodies.)

Indeed, there is a phenomenon, within the purview of a distinct although marginal sociological speciality, which as Rose and Rose write in a standard text, is "the flip side of the record [of] social control." This is "deviance," literally a turning aside, swerving. "When social control fails, people violate some standards of behavior generally accepted by society."[25]

Now culturally, at least in the modern age—and Mills writes that the task of social science in our day is above all cultural—deviance is the bearer of glad tidings. It is cultural innovation. But in sociology, overwhelmingly, it is an embarrassing footnote, an anomaly, a failure, although Rose and Rose write that some sociologists regard "some deviance . . . as a harbinger of social change, dependent at least in part upon changes in the technology or structure of the society."[26] Irving Louis Horowitz, a devoted follower of Mills (and a follower also of Howard Becker, Mills' teacher at Wisconsin, who wrote the book *The Outsiders*), is one of the few sociologists to treat deviance as part of the *political* process, an approach congruent with both the politics of black, Latin, and white youth movements in recent years, and the older types of "primitive rebellion" (banditry, etc.) now being researched by such scholars as Eric Hobsbawm. Thus Horowitz writes, sharpening the issue from a Millsian point of view, that in politicized deviance, "change would be initiated from below by members of subordinate marginal groups. This would be in sharp contrast to the conventional elitist pattern of politics, where decisions are made from above by members of the prevailing majority."[27]

But the *why* of deviance, *why* the atoms swerve, is left unexplained. Indeed, perhaps it cannot be explained by the bourgeois "science of society" (although the bourgeoisie comes into existence because of it). Marx writes abstractly—and in the "dialogue with Marx," which according to Mills and others underlies the history of sociology, this idea is never really confronted. Social change occurs when "exisiting social relations have come into conflict with the existing force of production."[28] And this, elliptically in Marx's text, parenthetically, is an affair of "The human body.' Need and labor."[29] More concretely, so far as the working-class movement is concerned, there is "a contradiction between the personality of each separate proletarian and labor, the condition of life forced upon him."[30] There is a contradiction between life and the historical conditions of life. More concretely still:

In countries like North America which begin in an already advanced historical epoch, development proceeds very rapidly. Such countries have not other natural premises than the individuals who settled there and were induced to do so because the forms of interaction in the old countries did not correspond to their wants. Thus they begin with the most advanced individuals of the old countries and with the correspondingly most advanced form of interaction, even before this form of interaction has been established in the old countries.[31]

It is because of some inner impetus, that the atoms, in conflict with a recalcitrant environment, swerve. The impetus in the individual is toward a new form of interaction among individuals—in short, a need, however "deviant," for community, a need opaque both to the dying Hellenistic world of Epicurus and our late bourgeois Imperium. (And a need apparently opaque also to Mills, who writes that "The cry for community" is a "mistaken attempt to overcome alienation.")[32]

The question in essence is no more answerable for Mills, the (increasingly) radical sociologist, than for Parsons, the conservative sociologist. As the philosopher Whitehead (also a great sociologist, and, simultaneously, a philosopher of "organism,") wrote, the question is how "novelty enters the world."[33] And Whitehead's answer, congruent with Marx, and also with Mills' deeper intuition, is that it is through "feeling": Marx's "human body, need and labor"; Mills' "sensibility," "culture." For in feeling there is inherently and always a "contrast" between "in fact" and "might be."

This quality of imagination, this contrast between "what is" and "what might be"—which as I suggest elsewhere is distinctive of every labor process, and *ipso facto* revolutionary—was doubtless part of Mills' personal method of scholarship, his "intellectual craftsmanship," as expounded in his Appendix to *The Sociological Imagination*. However, it is not until the book on Cuba, that it may be seen to dominate his social thought, so that the contrast, indeed, is more between "what is" and "what *was*"; "cherished values" and "threats" to those values. Although there are strong contrary currents, the "program" of Mills' sociological imagination tends on the whole to be more Wittgensteinian than Marxist, therapeutic in the superficial sense; it is clarification, illumination, awareness. "Translating personal troubles into public issues," as Mills so often emphasizes, it serves primarily not action, but debate. It creates the "publics" which as we have seen dominate Mills' imagination so strongly. Otherwise, like Wittgenstein's therapeutics, it leaves things pretty much as before; or more precisely, restores a more humane, more "humanistic," *status quo ante*.

Mao Tse-tung writes, in accents which Mills, through the medium of his Cuban revolutionary, will shortly adopt:

> So many deeds cry out to be done,
> And always urgently;
> The world rolls on,
> Time presses.
> Ten thousand years are too long,
> Seize the day, seize the hour!

Mills writes:

It is the political task of the social scientist—as of any liberal educator—continually to translate personal troubles into public issues, and public issues into the terms of their human meaning for a variety of individuals. . . . What we represent—although this is not always apparent—is man become aware of mankind. It its on the level of human awareness that virtually all solutions to the great problems must now lie.[34]

In a short while, much will have changed, and Mills' solution to our great solutions will no longer lie merely on the level of human awareness, but—Listen, Yankee!—in insurrection, revolution. To be sure, revolution may also lie on the level of human awareness. But the temperature of that awareness has got to be heated up quite a bit, heated, perhaps "unreasonably," to the boiling point.

LISTEN, YANKEE!
So it seems to us, you're up against this:
You've got to make your Government change its whole line of policy, you've got to argue for a completely new United States approach to the problems of the hungry world.
But to do that you've got to change drastically the whole economic system of your big corporations, at least as they operate outside the U.S.A.
You've got to smash Yankee imperialism from inside the United States. For you can't hope to make your Government—if it is your Government—change its line of policy unless you do smash that system.[35]

We Cuban revolutionaires don't really know just exactly *how* you could best go about this transformation of your Yankee imperialism. For us, with our problems, it was simple: In Cuba, we had to take our "Rocky Mountains"—you couldn't do that, could you? Not yet, we suppose.
(We're joking—we suppose. But if in ten years, in five years—if things go as we think they might inside your country, if it comes to that, then know this, Yankee: some of us will be with you. God almighty, those are great mountains!)[36]

But we are not yet in the mountains. We are still at the stage, as Marx writes (to take up the dialogue again), of criticism. Our "essential pathos is *indignation*, [our] essential task, *denunciation*."

It is a matter of describing the pervasive, suffocating pressure of all social spheres on one another, the general but passive dejection, the narrowness that recognizes but misunderstands itself—this framed in a system of government that lives on the conservation of all meanness and is nothing but *meanness in government*.[37]

In defense of this suffocating social order, whose zenith in our day is Nixonism (which we may take to designate a kind of politics not confined to the administration of Richard M. Nixon), Parsons elaborates, as Gouldner writes, a theory of "Structural-Functionalism," of "system equilibrium," a theory of society as "a self-maintaining homeostatic system."[38] And this, originally, in

a time of mass meetings, marches, demonstrations, shotgun auctions, protests, petitions, welfare demands, militant organizations, street corner meetings, and riots: it was a time of widespread collective unrest. From the conservative standpoint such a period is viewed as an acute threat to social order; from a radical standpoint, however, the time may be seen as one of revolutionary opportunity. The problem of social order, then, is the conservative's way of talking about the conditions when an established elite is unable to rule in traditional ways and when there is a crisis of the master institutions.[39]

As Mills writes:

In these terms, the idea of conflict cannot effectively be formulated. . . . The magical elimination of conflict, and the wondrous achievement of harmony, remove from this "systematic" and "general" theory the possibilities of dealing with social change, with history. Not only does the "collective behavior" of terrorized masses and excited mobs, crowds and movements—with which our era is so filled—find no place in the normatively created social structure of grand theorists. But any systematic ideas of how history itself occurs, of its mechanics and processes, are unavailable to grand theory, and accordingly, Parsons believes, unavailable to social science: "When such a theory is available the millenium for social science will have arrived. This will not come in our time and most probably never." Surely this is an extraordinarily vague assertion.[40]

Similarly, "abstracted empiricism," the second front on which Mills fights against establishment social science, is a "withdrawal from the tasks of the social sciences." Parallel to "the fetishism of the concept," in grand theory, is abstracted empiricism's "methodological inhibition," which yields a "microscopic" perspective, a perspective "in which all problems are seen as a scatter of requests for scattered information, statistical or otherwise, about a scatter of individuals and their scattered milieux."[41]

What social theory needs, in its concern with method, is not pseudo-scientific "inhibition" (a notion which has a special existential meaning for Mills, who early struggled to break out of the Cartesian circle, in large measure defined by Descartes' "Discourse on Method") but "release": "the release rather than the restriction of the sociological imagination."[42]

Indeed, even in the physical sciences, on which abstracted empiricism professes to model itself, discovery issues not from the rigid epistemological scruples of positivistic philosophers, but from the free play of imagination, "with no holds barred" (as Mills quotes the physicist Percy Bridgman). Indeed, as a new school of philosophers is teaching us, the great advances in science, the great conceptual revolutions, have come from the very same "big connection" between fantasy and reality that defines social revolution. They come, as the popularizer Arthur Koestler writes, from "the sleep walkers."

As Mills writes:

The classic social analyst has avoided any rigid set of procedures; he has sought to develop and to use in his work the sociological imagination. Repelled by the association and disassociation of Concepts, he has used more elaborated terms only when he has good reason to believe that by their use he enlarges the scope of his sensibilities, the precision of his references, the depth of his reasoning. He has not been inhibited by method and technique; the classic way has been the way of the intellectual craftsman.[43]

What Mills fails fully to realize, or at least to keep consistently in sight, although it is implicit in the sociological imagination itself, is that this "release" comes not to the unattached craftsman, working in privatistic solitude, but, as Mills also says, to the "cultural workman," in solidarity with other useful workers; in solidarity with human nature as it objectifies itself in the cultural-economic process. Once again, there are no individualistic, privatistic, solutions to our personal troubles, not even that, so often invoked, so desperately pursued, of the independent craftsman. Once again, the so-called Jeffersonian ideal dies hard with Mills. It consumes his energies and divides him against his deeper intuition. For as Marx writes:

Even as I am *scientifically* active, etc.—an activity I can seldom pursue in direct community with others—I am *socially* active because I am active as a *man*. Not only is the material of my activity—such as the language in which the thinker is active—given me as a social product, but my *own* existence *is* social activity; what I make from myself I make for society, conscious of my nature as social.[44]

Once again, styles of reflection are definitions of reality. The style of the independent craftsman, the frontier style, is an elitist style and defines reality as essentially elitist, either "one man, one rifle," or power elites, and never broad masses. Similarly, as Mills writes, abstracted empiricism defines its own reality: "Any style of empiricism involves a metaphysical choice—a choice as to what is most real—and now we must see something of the choice required by this personal style."[45] It is the paradox of abstracted empiricism, as a style of social thought, that it effectively denies the reality of society; or as Mills writes, "rests upon an explicit metaphysical denial of the reality of social structure," and more precisely, "historical social structure."[46] Its assumption is, "that the institutional structure of society, in so far as it is to be studied in this way, can be understood by means of . . . data about individuals,"[47] understood by means of "abstracted, statistical information about a series of contemporary individuals."[48] That is to say, in terms of the controversies in which Mills was immersed in his pragmatist days—the controversies of Peirce, James, and Dewey, which work themselves out fatefully, dialectically, throughout Mills' life—abstracted empiricism is nominalistic.

The fruit of this nominalism, socially, is first "the liberal practicality," the piece-meal reform of small milieux and then, "the illiberal practicality": the bureaucratic ethos, human relations, social engineering—indeed, the bureaucratization of social science itself, which should be "the prime carrier of freedom and reason in human affairs"[49] but instead serves the enemies of freedom and reason, serves, as we have seen, "bureaucratic forms of domination in modern society."[50]

In the academy, Mills' base of operations, there comes to prevail, over the "old-fashioned professor," working as a craftsman, "the idea of a university as a set of research bureaucracies, each containing an elaborate division of labor, and hence of intellectual technicians."[51] And among those technicians—and here is another surrealist motif, recalling Breton's denunciation of those "who use their minds as they would a savings bank"[52]—"intelligence itself is often dissociated from personality, and is seen by them as a kind of skillful gadget that they hope to market successfully. They are among the humanistically impoverished, living with reference to values that exclude any arising from a respect from human reason."[53]

Now Columbia, Mills' base of operations, once again, is as Jacques Barzun has said, "run like a bank." How should it be run? Here Mills' own "idea of a university" and his sense of himself as a university man come into focus. The new idea of a university, as we have seen, is of a research bureaucracy. The old idea which it replaces, and which Mills apparently espouses, is of "a circle of professional peers, each with apprentices and each practicing a craft."[54] About this, there is nothing radical. And indeed, although Mills links his critique of bureaucratic social science and the bureaucratic university (and social science, as the prime carrier of humanistic values in our time, is presumably the heart of the university) to the "dominant trends of modern social structure," the vicissitudes of the academy are effectively isolated from social structure and society at large. Thus, he does not account for the Marxist ascendancy which began among *students* of radical sociology, philosophy, anthropology, etc., and which Mills lived just long enough to glimpse, in the very heart of the bureaucratic style.

This idea of the university touches on the very core of Mills' project as a social scientist, as it does on humanistic culture generally. It touches on the very core of the question of "freedom and reason," Mills' "cherished values." Yet on this question of the idea of a university—and Mills spent most of his life in university life—Mills is at best ambiguous. Paul Goodman, both a traditionalist and an innovator, writes of "the community of scholars," whose essential activity is "teaching-and-learning." And this may well be Mills' "circle of professional peers and their apprentices." But as Goodman goes on to say, "The idea of education is to bring up the young to be new centers of initiative; they are not merely trainees."[55] Here—and this is the issue of language, publics, the man of knowledge, etc., which runs throughout Mills' life and work, and above all the issue of elites—Mills strikes a somewhat different note:

Teaching, by the way, I do not regard as altogether in the same case as writing. When one publishes a book it becomes a public property; the author's only responsibility to his reading public, if any, is to make it as good a book as he can and he is the final judge of that. But the teacher has further responsibilities. To some extent, students are a captive audience, and to some extent they are dependent upon their teacher, who is something of a model to them. His foremost job is to reveal to them as fully as he can just how a supposedly self-disciplined mind works. The art of teaching is in considerable part the art of thinking out loud but intelligibly. In a book the writer is often trying to persuade others of the results of his thinking; in a classroom the teacher ought to be trying to show others how one man thinks—and at the same time reveal what a fine feeling he gets when he does it well.[56]

Now even in the case of books, what Mills says here is questionable. For if writing a book, of any kind, fiction or nonfiction, is not teaching, what good is it? And to teach is surely not merely to try to persuade others of one's own views, nor is it to display one's self-disciplined mind; but rather (as Mills would probably agree in principle) to raise questions, invite dialogue. It is *speech*, once again, but in the interrogative not the indicative mood. (It is not *making* a speech.) This is how we become, as Mills writes, "self-cultivating, self-educating" men and women. And this is the way of all education, cultivation, development; the way, indeed, as we have had occasion earlier to remark, of organic evolution itself, the issue which so preoccupied the founders of pragmatism. For the environment, always changing, puts questions to the organism in it, who either responds creatively and makes the leap into the future, or declines and perishes.

And this brings us to the question of freedom and reason:

No problem can be adequately formulated unless the values involved and the apparent threat to them are stated. These values and their imperilment constitute the terms of the problem itself. The values that have been the thread of classic social analysis, I believe, are freedom and reason; the forces that imperil them today seem at times to be co-extensive with the major trends of contemporary society, if not to constitute the characteristic features of the contemporary period. The leading problems of the social studies today have this in common; they concern conditions and tendencies that seem to imperil these two values and the consequences of that imperilment for the nature of man and the making of history.[57]

Now in one sense, Mills is fighting an essentially rear-guard action here. He is fighting to preserve *traditional* values. For these values, "involved in the cultural problem of individuality," "are conveniently embodied in all that is suggested by the ideal of the Renaissance man."[58] This effort, if it is such, to restore the *status quo ante*, is surely not the creative response of the troubled organism in the environment.

On the other hand, "we are now at the ending of an epoch, and we have got to work out our own answers."[59] We must, in our leap into the future, into the new epoch, create new values—the values, as it were, no longer of fins but of legs, no longer of gills but of lungs (or more precisely, for legs and lungs are *organs* of development, of land life rather than sea life).

But what if this very leap into the future is a dead end, living fossilization, Weberian "petrifaction"—or as Mills so often says, the cheerful robot: "The ideological mark of the Fourth Epoch—that which sets it off from the Modern Age—is that the ideas of freedom and of reason have become moot; that increased rationality may not be assumed to make for increased freedom. . . . The major development of our time, I believe, can be correctly understood neither in terms of the liberal nor marxian interpretation of politics and culture."[60]

Here the Weberian pessimism comes to the fore, the pessimism, as Gerth and Mills write, of a "nostalgic liberal, feeling himself on the defensive";[61] the pessimism of "rationality without reason" and of "rationally organized social arrangements [which] are not necessarily a means of increased freedom for the individual or for the society."[62]

What is this "rationality without reason," and what, indeed, are these ideas of freedom and reason which have become moot? Gerth and Mills write, "The principle of rationalization is the most general element in Weber's philosophy of history."[63] Stating that socially, rationalization is efficient organization, usually bureaucratic, and this proceeds even more comprehensively and pervasively in socialism than in capitalism. "Weber . . . identifies bureaucracy with rationality, and the process of rationalization with mechanism, depersonalization, and oppressive routine."[64]

Nevertheless, Weber distinguishes between "formal rationality," which is the calculated means, especially economic, for achieving ends, and "substantive rationality," which "cannot be measured in terms of formal calculation alone, but also involves a relation to the absolute values or to the content of the particular given ends to which it is oriented."[65] It is thus that Mills attempts to distinguish between "functionally rational bureacracies" and "a society in which human reason were widely and democratically installed."[66]

Now this problem, the great problem, which has agitated modern ethicists and social thinkers, of means and ends, is in both Weber and Mills framed in a rather peculiar way; peculiar in the same sense as Weber's definition of the state, in terms of its "means." For as

Herbert Marcuse has pointed out, "the apparatus, which dictates its own objective administration," i.e., the apparatus constructed by Weber's formal rationality, "is itself instrument, means—and there is no such thing as a means 'as such.' Even the most productive, most reified apparatus is a means to an end outside itself."[67] Thus, once again, in a peculiarly German sense, "the value-free rationality of administration is dependent upon values and goals that come to it from outside," namely, as Marcuse goes on, glossing Weber, from "the power politics of the nation-state," i.e., "*imperialism.*"[68]

If we go still further "outside"—toward absolute *irrationality*, manifested either as "infinite regress," or more practically as "charismatic authority," we come to the peculiarly German cult of the Leader. After all, we must act for the sake of something, and Weber's theory is above all else a theory of *social action.* In short, in this theory of rationality, reason has no *rationale* (although Talcott Parsons disingenuously writes that "the role of ultimate values as the direct goals of chains of action is completely clear in Weber's work").[69]

The issue, then, from which the whole of sociology hangs suspended, is one of values—an issue, perhaps, more of art than of science, more of choice than calculation. Given a rational determination of *means,* the question at hand—the great question of modern post-dogmatic ethical theory; the question, as Dewey wrote, of "the Construction of the Good"—is whether there can be a rational determination of *ends* and, in the present instance, a rational critique of "functionally rational" bureaucratic society.

Reason, indeed, might better be called a procedure which mediates values for subjects striving to attain them. But Mills writes, in terms which seem poorly thought out and largely rhetorical, that, along with freedom, reason is a value. Pragmatically, it is the problem-solver, which as Marx writes, "meets at each step fresh problems to solve"; as Mills recognizes, it is practicality—liberal or illiberal, depending on the uses to which it is put. Thus there are bureaucratic uses of reason and humanistic uses of reason—for example, in administering a university—and if we are obliged to state the grounds of our choice, we may perhaps simply say with Marx that the root is man and that our use of reason must be manly and womanly. (Thus, as Marcuse writes, "capitalist rationality abstracts from man, to whose needs it is indifferent.")[70] Mills also recognizes that the question is then one of "what type of person" we want to promote and let prevail in our society. And this, perhaps, is a question no longer of ethical theory, conventionally construed, but, as Mills comes more and more to insist, of culture (in German, *Bildung,* Dewey's quasi-esthetic "construction"). Thus Mills writes that "in our time, what is at issue is the very nature of man, the image we have of his limits and possibilities as man."[71]

And this issue for Mills, is not easily resolved: "It will no longer do merely to assume, as a metaphysics of human nature, that down deep in man-as-man there is an urge for freedom and a will to reason."[72] That is to say, this will not do as an *assumption.* And yet, it is not a mere assumption but, as it were, the direct deliverance of our senses, the incontestable evidence of the sociological imagination itself; for we know that man in bureaucratic society is troubled, that he is "increasingly self-rationalized and increasingly uneasy."[73] And we know, although Mills writes that "the cry for community is a mistake," that this is a social problem, a problem of "social structure." Once again, as at the beginning: "Nowadays men often feel that their private lives are a series of traps. . . . Underlying this sense of being trapped are seemingly impersonal changes in the very structure of continent-wide societies."[74].

What, then, is Mills' problem? "Back of all this there lies the simple and decisive fact that alienated man is the antithesis of the Western image of the free man."[75] But this Mills fears, may only be an *image,* no more true or no less illusory, than the bureaucratic image of man; it may, that is, be merely "sociological." Who is to say that the cheerful robot is not as much of a "man," as fully *human,* as the Renaissance man, or the Marxian man?

This question, which Mills clearly agonizes over, is perhaps unanswerable. But like sociological pollsters, let us ask the cheerful robot himself:

We know of course that man can be turned into a robot, by chemical and psychiatric means, by steady coercion and by controlled environment; but also by random pressures and unplanned sequences of circumstances. But can he be made to want to become a cheerful and willing robot? Can he be happy in this condition, and what are the qualities and the meaning of such happiness? . . . Now we must ask: What in man's nature, what in the human condition today, what in each of the varieties of social structure makes for the ascendance of the cheerful robot? And what stands against it?[76]

Are *you* free, are *you* happy? (As earlier, Are the rich free and happy?) The question seems to turn, indeed, on this matter of happiness (for the one-time labor theoretician, the independent Leftist, who wanted men to be free and joyous); on happiness and its reality or unreality; on true and false consciousness; on essence and appearance; once again, on the *definition* of reality, revolutionary or reactionary, happy or unhappy; indeed, after all, on a metaphysics of nature and human nature. It is, as we shall see in our final chapter, on these simple, existential questions that Marxism stands or falls, and that Mills stands or falls as a radical social thinker. For above all else, Marx's revolutionary consciousness constitutes an absolute commitment to happiness. Thus, "Criticism has plucked imaginary flowers from the chain, not so that man will wear the chain that is without fantasy or consolation, but so that he will throw it off and pluck the living flower."[77] This, I believe, is in accord with our fundamental intuition, the fundamental experience which is for pragmatism the touch stone of reality and unreality, in us and outside us; the fundamental intuition which surges up at last in Mills' book on revolutionary Cuba, *Listen Yankee!*

CHAPTER 7

# Marxism Revisited: New Beginnings

THE endemic and perpetual crisis of sociology itself, which comes to a head in the final confrontation with Marx, is adumbrated in Mills' anthology of 1960, *Images of Man; The Classic Tradition in Sociological Thinking*. For although Mills begins with the "study of man," this study yields, after all, no "image of man" but only "models of society"—in terms which are really quite obscure and unspecifiable, in the way that an image of man may be specifiable. "It is these models that are great—not only as contributions to the history of social reflection and inquiry, but also as influences on subsequent sociological thinking. They, I believe, are what is alive in the classic tradition of sociology."[1]

It is no wonder, then, that there is a "crisis of individuality" and a "moral crisis of the humanist tradition, reflected in sociology, . . ."[2] For there can be no anchoring of humanism, in the dialectic of man and society, if there is no concept of the human.

To be sure, this dialectic is a tricky business, just as much, perhaps, in Marx, for whom, as he writes against "the essence of man . . . is the ensemble of social relations"[3]; as for the other social thinkers whom Mills admires. And yet, as we shall try to make clear, there is in Marx—as there is not in Weber whom Mills pairs with Marx as "the two sociologists who stand up above all the rest"—an image of man which resists all sociological socialization, stratification, rationalization, and so forth.

Thus, if for the pessimistic Weber, as we have seen, history is the history of rationalization, dehumanization (if indeed there is anything essentially human to be dehumanized); for Marx—both Marx and Weber, as Mills writes, being "soaked in knowledge of history"— "the whole of what is called world history is nothing but the creation of man himself by human labor."[4]

135

Indeed, as Robert Nisbet writes (although not, perhaps, with sufficient attention to the nuances), there is throughout Marx an unyielding faith in "the existential reality of man":

We speak often of Marx's "social" conception of the nature of human personality, contrasting it with the conception of man that is to be seen in the writings of the classical economists of his day. But it would be a mistake to assume from this that Marx's view of the nature of man is social in the sense that we find, say, in Durkheim—or even in Weber and Simmel. For all Marx's historical sense of social organizations and of the shifting manifestations of human types—slave, serf, proletarian, and so on—there is nevertheless an unwavering acceptance of the stability and reality of the human being. The root is man![5]

Indeed, it is definitive of much sociology that there is no root. And as we shall see more clearly later, this may be the key to the great issue of "stratification," which so sorely excercises Mills: stratification by "class," as in Marx, or by "status," "status honor," as in Weber. For the history which is the creation of man himself by human labor, according to Marx, is also the history of class struggle; whereas we would be loathe to say that human history is the history, as a latterday Weberian writes, of status seeking. (That Weber himself concedes priority to the Marxian model is clear: e.g., "Every technological repercussion and economic transformation threatens stratification by status and pushes the class situation into the foreground. Epochs and countries in which the naked class situation is of predominant significance are regularly the periods of technological and economic transformations.")[6]

Thus Mills writes of Marx that "A positive image of man, of what man might come to be, lies under every line of his analysis of what he held to be an inhuman society."[7] And without this image there can be no social criticism; for we know it, as Bergson wrote, by its power of negation. And yet the image, the icon, has been shattered. Mills lacks this Marxian faith in man, the faith that defines Marx's radicalism— for radicalism, "radix," goes to root, and, as Nisbet reminds us, for Marx "the root is man." He therefore characterizes Marxism as a nineteenth-century philosophy and writes: "Both Marxism and liberalism bear the marks of a period of human history that is ending."[8] For Marxism shares with liberalism the ideals of "the humanist tradition," the ideals of "freedom and reason," and as we have seen in our own epoch, the Fourth Epoch, these ideals have become moot.

Nevertheless, in his book on Marx, Mills, the transplanted Texas radical, does struggle to get back to his own roots and comes round full circle, the better, perhaps, to make a new beginning. For in Marxism, ideas matter, and ideas have consequences: ". . . regardless of motive and use, ideas have mattered to the marxists and, in one or another, these ideas are derived from what Karl Marx wrote."[9] And these Marxist ideas are saving ideas, ideas to be preached. "Little wonder that clergymen regularly complain that the communists "have stolen our stuff." Indeed, Marxism as ideology is less a message than a "gospel," which in the literal sense means "glad tidings."[10] What are these glad tidings of Marxism for which Mills, who early wished men to be enthusiastic and joyous, assumes the role of preacher?

You do not have to be poor any longer. . . . You are poor not because of anything you have done or anything you have failed to do, not because of Original Sin or the Will of God or because of bad luck. You are poor because of economic and political conditions. These conditions are called capitalism. The conditions that made you poor can be changed. They are going to be changed. Inside capitalism itself are the seeds of its own destruction. What will happen, whether you are yet aware of it or not, is that you are going to make a revolution. . . . By the revolution you can eliminate once and for all the exploitation of man by man; you can enter into a socialist society in which mankind conquers nature. And no man any longer will know poverty and exploitation.[11]

Thus, "In marxism, ideal and agency, theory and ideology can be very closely connected, . . ."[12] Here again, is the big unity—idea and action, theory and practice—which Mills sought at the beginning of his career; sought in pragmatism, where, as we have seen, Dewey vies with Marx as an exemplar of the unity of theory and practice; sought in the labor movement, the alliance, as Mills hoped, of intellect and social action, mind and muscle, and finally, perhaps, despaired of. For in liberalism, at any rate, the ideals of the humanist tradition, to which Mills so often pays homage, "have been increasingly divorced from any historical agencies by which they might be realized. . . . That is one reason liberalism is now more of a rhetoric than anything else."

It is doubtful that liberalism is in a position to designate the conditions under which the ideals it proclaims might be realized. It has been detached from any tenable theory of society and from any effective means of action. Accordingly, however engaging as a set of ideals, even these ideals in their abstracted and formal condition are no longer useful as guidelines to judgments about what is going on in the world, or as guidelines for those who would by the will of men consciously modify the course of historical events.[13]

In other words, in terms of Mills' theory of politics, which he elaborates in his earliest writings on language and never abandons, liberalism has no "public." The Marxist gospel, however, is in a different situation.

To understand this gospel, one must understand whom it attracts. The big answer to that question today is: It attracts many intelligent and alert people in the impoverished countries. Most of the world's population live in such hungry countries, and these countries are now very much in commotion. There is no longer any "unchanging East," no "primitively static Africa," no Latin America sitting in stupor in the sun. Their peoples are clamoring for the fruits of industrialization, and with good historical reason many reject the capitalist way of achieving them. Several varieties of marxism are among the modes of industrialization available to them.[14]

This is the Marxism of "hunger," as Mills writes, the Marxism of what has come to be called the Third World. But it is not, Mills writes, the Marxism of Marx, who expected revolution to come in the world of advanced capitalism, with the industrial working class, the proletariat, as its "historical agency." Thus, "Marx's major political expectation about advanced capitalism has collapsed: the central agency which he designated has not developed as expected; the role he expected that agency to enact has not been enacted."[15] The premise of these disappointments, which once, we may suspect, broke Mills' heart, is the erroneous "labor metaphysic," and from the labor metaphysic stem the main errors of Marxism:

Behind the labor metaphysic and the erroneous views of its supporting trends there are deficiencies in the marxist categories of stratification; ambiguities and misjudgments about the psychological and political consequences of the development of the economic base; errors concerning the supremacy of economic causes within the history of societies and the mentality of classes; inadequacies of a rationalist psychological theory; a generally erroneous theory of power; an inadequate conception of the state.[16]

It is apparent that Mills is here trying to ride two theses at once, one Marxist or quasi-Marxist, the Marxism of the Third World, and the other anti-Marxist. The latter plainly refutes, unhorses, Marx: the industrial working class has not become an "agency" of revolution but has been integrated into capitalism. The former, as developed in the wake of the Leninist theory of imperialism, reasons that as "Imperialism is a global strategy," so is revolution. Thus it globalizes the class struggle, so that the backward, colonial world stands in the position of revolutionary proletariat to the capitalist-imperialist nations. To this degree Mills continues to have revolutionary expectations—witness the book on Cuba—and continues in the spirit of Marxism.

But Mills never really confronts Lenin's Marxist interpretation of the failure of revolutionary expectations in the capitalist world—Marxist at least in the sense of "social existence determining consciousness," in the sense of "economic causes." As Lenin writes:

The receipt of high monopoly profits by the capitalists in one of the numerous branches of industry,, in one of the numerous countries, etc., makes it economically possible for them to corrupt certain sections of the working class, and for a time a fairly considerable minority, and win them to the side of the bourgeoisie of a given industry or nation against all the others. The intensification of antagonisms between imperialist nations for the division of the world increases this striving. And so there is created that bond between imperialism and opportunism, which revealed itself first and most clearly in England owing to the fact that certain features of imperialist development were observable there much earlier than in other countries.[17]

Rather than this "materialist" interpretation, in which the working class in capitalist countries is bought off by the "super-profits" derived from exploitation of the underdeveloped world, Mills prefers an "idealistic" one: the Weberian inversion of the Marxist formula, in which consciousness, through the "cultural apparatus," "the ideological superstructure," determines social existence. "Existence itself is subject to the definitions of reality carried by the cultural apparatus. Consciousness itself, even self-identity, is also subject to these stereotypes and meanings."[18]

This, the manipulation of "consciousness," is of course the leading premise of the greater part of Mills' work and of much sociology. Thus Mills writes of Marx's "rationalist psychology," his "rationalist model of ideological forms and class consciousness." "He seems to believe that class consciousness is a necessary psychological consequence of objective economic development, which includes the polarization of owners and workers."[19]

This is a fundamental, although very prevalent, misunderstanding of Marx. "Class consciousness" (a term of quite limited use in the

Marxist texts) is by no means Marx's leading premise. Rather, it is illusory consciousness, precisely, false consciousness, ideology, mystification—religiosity, in the broadest sense—that he first of all takes up arms against; and he fights not only intellectually and ideally, but materially, in solidarity with the proletariat, the "material weapon" of history. Thus Mills characterizes Marx as a rationalist thinker and at the same time quotes the passage which refutes this rationalism: "To demand that men should abandon illusions about their condition is to demand that a condition that needs illusions should itself be abandoned."[20]

For the beginning of criticism, and of revolutionary action, as Marx writes, is the criticism of religion and illusion; for religion is "the opium of the people." Rationalism, indeed, is not the issue here. Rather, it is "vitalism"; for religion dulls the senses, benumbs the body. Marx writes: "The criticism of religion disillusions man so that he thinks, acts, and shapes his reality like a disillusioned man who has come to his senses, so that he revolves around himself and thus around his own true sun."[21] It is the crux of the revolution to unfetter the body, the human body, human sensuousness, man's "physical organization," as Marx writes, which is both the work of all history, and the first premise of history. This Marx stresses again and again, throughout his writings. It is the indispensable materialism, the somatism, as we have said (anti-somatists take notice!), of radical social thought and action:

> The first premise of all human history, of course, is the existence of living human individuals. . . . The first fact to be established, then, is the physical organization of these individuals and their consequent relationship to the rest of nature.[22]

> In dealing with Germans devoid of premises, we must begin by stating the first premise of all human existence, and hence of all history, the premise, namely, that men must be able to live in order to be able "to make history." . . . But life involves above all eating and drinking, shelter, clothing, and many other things . . . The first principle therefore in any theory of history is to observe this fundamental fact in its entire significance and all its implications and to attribute to this fact its due importance.[23]

Thus the Marxist formula, "Consciousness does not determine life, but life determines conciousness"—which Mills, following Weber, is inclined to invert—is no mere matter of the chicken or the egg but absolutely indispensable. For consciousness can be endlessly deceived; but the body, the material life process, practical need—

nature, in short—cannot. Thus, as Herbert Marcuse and others have argued, the revolutionary struggle takes place essentially in the sphere of sensuousness—the sphere, indeed, of Eros. It is as history advances, an essentially religious struggle, a struggle against the "priestly nature," as Marx writes, the priestly influence which anesthetizes the body (a struggle which follows a dialectical, zigzag course: hence the "sexual revolution" in both its positive and negative aspects): ". . . if Protestantism was not the true solution, it was the true formulation of the problem. The question was no longer the struggle of the layman against the *priest external to him* but of his struggle against *his own inner priest,* his *priestly nature.*"[24]

This struggle, indeed, inheres in the historical process itself, the process of the developing productive forces (a process which although independent of the *will* of men, is yet their own process of self-formation, of growth, which of course cannot be willed). For the productive forces are essentially the energies of the human body, the first premise of all history; and as history proceeds, the human body becomes ever more fitted for many things, as we have said, and correspondingly, ever more needy. (This fact is entirely consistent with an absolute growth in social and individual wealth, conventionally measured: for "The rich man is simultaneously one who needs a *totality* of human manifestations of life and in whom his own realization exists as inner necessity, as need."[25]

That is, the historical process, and especially capitalism, its penultimate phase, creates a human individual, fitted for many things *which are denied him.* And the class of such individuals—the class with "radical chains," as Marx writes, "radical needs"—is the proletariat: the hungry, needy class in the broadest sense, regardless of its living standard, conventionally conceived.

It is indeed, Marx believed, a law of history, historical nature, social nature that capitalism, the system that polarizes society into buyers and sellers of labor—and this is the dynamic of all wage labor, both blue collar and white collar—should create such a class, an aggregate of people who say "No!" to capitalism and "Yes!" to socialism. The capitalism which offends human nature cultivates at the same time a human nature which will rebel against it. It "cultivates the five senses, lays bare the body's flesh."

There is thus a "contradiction" in the life-process, both of property owners and non-property owners, but in the first instance of non-property owners. For the non-property owner lives from wages, that is, he must alienate his labor in order to sustain his life, which is to say, alienate his essence, his life, himself; contradict himself, negate himself. (The capitalist and the landlord live from property, from profits and rent, respectively, and are also in contradiction with themselves: hence the indispensability of the property criterion for the analysis of social stratification.) For labor, according to the labor metaphysic which Marx espouses—productive life, life activity— belongs to the laborer as his essence, or, to put it somewhat differently, as an essential predicate.

Thus, in wage labor, the predicate is in contradiction with the subject. Once again, there is a contradiction in the life-process of the worker. But in order for the predicate to be in contradiction with the subject, there must *be* a subject, that is, in accordance with the materialist requirements of Marxist social analysis, an *embodied* subject, a live human animal.

And this is where "class consciousness" and "false consciousness" come in. Consciousness, according to Marx, is first of all the consciousness of the "mental laborers," the non-workers; it is "consciousness in a position to emancipate itself from the world."[26] As such, it is priestly consciousness, consciousness divorced from need. ("The first form of ideologists, *priests,* is concurrent.")[27] On the one hand, therefore, it is false consciousness, on the other, true consciousness, the true consciousness of the exploiter who does not satisfy his needs himself but lives from the labor of others. This is an evident contradiction in the life-process of ths exploiters, who nevertheless organize themselves as a class to maintain it. The unorganized workers, so long as they remain unorganized, maintain both the contradiction in their own life-process and in that of the non-workers.

Now the consciousness of the workers, whether or not it is organized as class consciousness, should, presumably, be "true consciousness," the consciousness of need, since they labor to fulfil need. (Thus, the crucial distinction philosophically, which must be overcome, is not so much between intellectual and "natural" labor as between the intellection which is of the body and the intellection which denies the body and which, since the thinker is an embodied subject, contradicts the subject.) Yet—and this is Mills' great animus against Marx, the theme of the greater part of his life's work, and his personal heartbreak—they are falsely conscious, their consciousness is also divorced from need. Why should this be? Why should they not feel the shoe that pinches? They are, in short, as Marx's criticism of religion indicates, desensitized to their own pain and misery. Theirs is indeed, as Marx writes, "a condition which requires illusions." And the stuff of their illusions? No longer literal religion, perhaps (although this still works it influence), but other forms of opium; automobiles, television, suburbia, etc.; dream stuff, in the pejorative sense as every one acknowledges. In short, desensitizing consumption patterns, "repressive consumption", as Stanley Aronowitz writes—or as Mills writes, once again, privatism.

Or we may go—still further and arrive at separatism. And this, once again, is the privatism, the idiot privatism, of separatism, the Jeffersonian scatter, the isolated monads. For we are separate no longer in our productive relations, no longer independent—a fact, as we have seen, which Mills is inclined to lament—but we remain, and become so increasingly, in patterns which sometimes seem to be deliberately contrived by the "Power Elite," separate in our social relations. Thus, in the present perspective, which may however change, and may already be changing, workers, as T.B. Bottomore emphasizes, "no longer have any collective aims," and "tend more and more to withdraw into private life."[28]

In a sense we are back where we started, bogged down in the mire of failed revolutionary hopes. It is a question of building a boat on the open sea: no revolution without class consciousness and no class consciousness without revolution. As Marx writes:

For the production of this communist consciousness on a mass scale and for the success of the cause itself, the alteration of men on a mass scale is required. This can only take place in a practical movement, in a *revolution*. A revolution is necessary, therefore, not only because the ruling class cannot be overthrown in any other way but also because the class overthrowing it can succeed only by revolution in getting rid of all the traditional muck and become capable of establishing society anew.[29]

And yet there is hope. For "This conception of history depends on our ability to set forth the real process of production, starting out from the material production of life itself, and to comprehend the form of interaction connected with this and created by this mode of production, that is, by civil society in its various stages, as the basis of all history."[30] "Starting out from the material production of life itself": that is, from the biological-cultural life-process, which must be sustained under any economic system, and which capitalism develops and constrains simultaneously—develops, indeed, "on a mass scale," altering, for both better and worse, dialectically, vast numbers of men and women.

Is there any evidence that this process is producing a revolutionary proletariat? Originally, in ancient Rome, the proletariat was the propertyless class, the class which contributes to society great numbers of offspring; more basically the "alimentary" class, hence the pre-eminent class both of production and reproduction, of nourishment and sexuality, or in a word, of *love*, the *erotic* class. This proletariat, we will remember, is the class with "radical chains" and "radical needs." It is the class which cannot live in bourgeois society, and can live, ultimately, only by overthrowing bourgeois society, i.e., radically transforming it in the direction of socialism. And it is a class, necessarily, compounded of many elements, of which the industrial proletariat, according to Marx's expectation, may be the leading element but not the sole element. That is to say, the class with radical chains, the proletariat, need not arise, at least not wholly, from the industrial working class. Marx believed that it is the logic of history that the class with radical chains should arise. But contrary, perhaps, to Marx's expectations—and even this is not altogether clear in Marx's writings—that class need not be the industrial working class as such. (Thus, as *The Communist Manifesto* itself says, "the proletariat is recruited from all classes of the population.")

Now logic aside, is there any evidence that a proletariat—a class of people who cannot live within bourgeois society, who are at the same time enlivened and exceedingly pained by it to the point of dropout, revolt, or very difficult, arduous, self-destructive coexistence—is forming in the United States. We have indeed, as we have already noted, lived through a decade of such evidence, of which Mills saw only the beginning—a decade encompassing sit-ins; freedom rides; ghetto riots; student strikes; rising alcoholism; child abuse; "consciousness expanding" drugs; terrorism; new forms of religion; and most significantly, perhaps, such labor movements as that of Cesar Chavez's Farm Workers, and such strikes as those at Farah clothing in Texas and at the General Motors plant at Lordstown, Ohio. As a sometime populist used to say, Let's look at the record: (as demonstrated in the following headlines from the New York Times over the period from 1970 to 1975).

Workers Increasingly Rebel Against Boredom on Assembly Line


Communes Are a Way of Life for Young Adults Seeking Revolution, God or Themselves

Communes Spread as the Young Reject Old Values

Marxist in Detroit Presses Class Struggle as a Judge

Lordstown—Searching for a Better Way of Work

Young Workers Disrupt Key G. M. Plant

American Ex-Nun Held By Bolivia as a Guerrilla

'Someday Us Poor Is Going to Overrule'

Now it is apparent—from "the record"—that none of these problems of poverty, crime, work morale, humane social services, social justice can be solved within the framework of bourgeois society. To this Mills would surely agree. But can they be solved at all in modern society? Mills replies:

> These . . . exploitations are not, we suspect, rooted in capitalism alone and as such. They are also coming about in non-capitalist and post-capitalist societies. They are not necessarily rooted either in the private ownership or in the state ownership of the means of production: they may be rooted in the facts of mass industrialization itself. [31]

This, in essence, is the answer to the question "Would communism make a difference?" Here, while by no means settling the question, let us look at another item reprinted on the "Op Ed" page of *The New York Times* from *Medical Opinion* (date and pp. to come) which deals with the Chinese approach (still not yet communist, we should remember) to drug addiction, not long ago a scourge of Chinese society and presently one of the darkest and most hopeless aspects of American urban life, in which a number of "social problems" are tied in a seemingly irresoluble knot.

### How China Solved the Drug Problem

#### By Paul Lowinger

DETROIT—Another country that once had an addiction problem—one that lasted for almost 200 years and involved an incredible 25 per cent of its population—is China.

Today China is virtually drug-free—and the method the Chinese used to eradicate their addiction problem might well offer methods we could use to achieve the same results.

China was forced into addiction by the Opium Wars. Contrary to popular belief, these wars—from 1839 to 1842—did not originate because China wanted to export opium. They began when China resisted England's demand to import opium in exchange for Chinese products—mostly tea, silk, and porcelain. China lost these wars, and among other indignities was forced to exchange its goods for opium. As a result it became a highly narcoticized country, a victim of ruthless Western economic and political policy. By 1850 an entire fifth of the revenue of the British Government of India—the source of opium—came from Chinese consumption of this drug.

Obviously to enlarge the market for opium, China was forced to create a huge number of addicts. And it did.

In October of 1949 the People's Republic of China was proclaimed. Within a year the Communist Government instituted a comprehensive program designed to eliminate this threat to the nation. All evidence indicates that by 1953 the problem of narcotic drug abuse was practically eliminated.

One important factor was the changed ideology of the young people—no new supply of addicts was forthcoming. The changes in outlook included a redefinition of the nation and its youth, of their worth and role. In rural areas this new definition was based on land distribution; collective farming; new educational, social and vocational opportunities; and the election of local councils. In the cities it took the form of rationalization of commerce and industry, full employment, worker control and the end of foreign domination.

This total ideological transformation of the younger generation was accompanied by the reintegration of Chinese society through small street committees that offered cultural leadership.

Equally significant in the Chinese drive to eliminate narcotic addiction were its methods of plugging the source. China is 80 per cent rural, and an unknown but significant part of the land had been turned into poppy cultivation. The first major economic and political mass campaign of the Government was land reform, and this aim was coordinated with elimination of poppy growth. Distribution of land from large landholders to landless peasants was accompanied by the need to convert the opium cash crops to badly needed food crops. Today China produces enough opium to meet its medical needs, but no more.

Smuggled opium was still a source of the drug, and China acted to stop this supply with a policy of "carrot and stick." Leniency was recommended for employees and workers of opium traffickers; but heavy penalties existed for those controlling the traffic, manufacture, or growth of opium.

China's attitude toward the individual reformed addict was one of goodwilled congratulations, and represents another important reason why the narcotic problem was overcome. The rehabilitation of opium addicts began with their registration. Arrangements by city-wide antiopium committees for addict rehabilitation included treatment to break the habit at home, in clinics and in hospitals.

At every stage of personal rehabilitation the ideological motivation was stressed. Given China's attitudes, this ideology was strong on political, social and economic information. But the important thing is that the anti-drug campaign recognized that the desire and will of the addict is ultimately the controlling factor of addiction. China's policy was not simply to deprive a person of drugs, but to replace the need for narcotics with a forceful, national commitment. Equally significant, the former addict was fully accepted back into Chinese life without official stigma or prejudice.

Naturally, many questions have to be answered about the total success of the Chinese experience. Is there an addict population living in labor camps or prisons because of failure to rehabilitate? Do the rehabilitated addicts all function as useful members of Chinese society? To what extent would addiction be a problem in China if its internal and border controls were less stringent? Does traditional Chinese medicine offer useful ideas about addiction treatment?

*Paul Lowinger, M.D., is adjunct professor of psychiatry at Wayne State University in Detroit. This article is excerpted from the monthly, Medical Opinion. (Reprinted with the permission of Medical Opinion)*

Here the writer stresses "idealistic motivation," that is, a sense of social purpose, embodied in the great masses and especially in the youth. This sense, Western socialists have long and quixotically argued, may be seen as a sense of a society for "people" and not for "profit." It is in this context that many problems of Chinese society have been solved, and it is in this context—consider General Motors—that we might go far toward raising morale and productivity, assuming useful productivity, in factories and offices (where drug abuse, even among people "gainfully employed," has been making inroads). This idealism, however, which the Chinese strongly emphasize, is not merely preached but has after all a "materialistic" basis—namely, the radical transformation, root and branch, geographically, demographically and socially, of the Chinese nation, in the process, as it is said, of building socialism. As recent Chinese experience and Mills' own deeper intuition, often expressed over the years, indicate, this is especially a transformation of "culture," a "cultural revolution." It is the question, as Mills often writes, of what kind of men and women will inherit the future. For production, rooted in the economic process, is ultimately the production of humanity itself. This, rather than any abstracted ideals, is Marx's humanism, the humanism of economism—and here Lenin, Georg Lukacs, Louis Altusser, and others could take a lesson. Thus Marx's image of the future is essentially an image of socialist man ("esthetic man," to sharpen the cultural perspective).

This makes Mills' repeated invocations of "tradition," the "moral tradition," and the "humanist tradition" somewhat questionable and his attribution to Marx of a place in this tradition somewhat inappropriate. Thus, "Considered morally, Karl Marx's principles are clearly among the animating principles of Western civilization."[32] Indeed, Marx frequently insists that unlike the utopian socialists, he proclaims no ideals, upholds no principles, which is to say, proclaims no abstract ideals, abstracted from the historical, socioeconomic process:

> Communism is for us not a stable state which is to be established, an ideal to which reality will have to adjust itself. We call communism the *real* movement which abolishes the present state of things. The conditions of this movement result from the premises now in existence.[33]

This Mills recognizes, but does not fully appreciate:

> The distinctive character of Marx's "scientific socialism," I think, lies in this: his images of the ideal society are connected with the actual workings of the society in which he lived. Out of his projections of the tendencies he discerns in society as it is actually developing he makes up his image of the future society (the post-capitalist society that he wants to come about). That is why he refuses, at least in his maturity, to *proclaim* ideals. Morally, of course, he condemns. Sociologically, he points to the results of that which he condemns. Politically, he directs attention to the agency of historical change—the proletariat—and he argues, with facts and figures, theories and slogans, that this developing connection between human agency and implicit goal is the most important trend in capitalist society. For by the development of this agency within it, capitalist society itself will be overthrown and socialism installed. The historical creation of the proletariat is the central thrust within the capitalist realm of necessity. That thrust is driving capitalism toward the revolutionary leap into the socialist epoch, into the realm of freedom.[34]

This is fine; nevertheless I remain puzzled; puzzled about these "tendencies," "actual workings," "trends," and especially—and here of course is the great stumbling block to Mills—about the efficacy of "the agency of historical change"; about the efficacy, indeed, of this whole "model of society," which, as we will remember, is the great thing in Marx. I remain, that is, as puzzled and unconvinced as Mills himself. For Mills does not really believe in "the revolutionary leap into the realm of freedom." He believes, rather, although surely with fear and trembling, as we have seen, in the advent of the cheerful robot. For the "model" he ascribes to Marx, of social "workings," is, in brief, *lifeless;* in these social workings, there is nothing which *works*, the way the sweaty proletariat, which Mills does not believe in, obviously works; there is no energy, of production and reproduction (for "energy," *ergon*, means "work"); there is no *physics*, where, as in a "physical model," *erg* is a unit of energy or work; no physics, from the Greek *phusikos*, "natural," from *phusis*, "nature" (related to *phulon*, a race, tribe, as in "phylum," and thus related to Marx's "species-being"), from *phuein*, to make grow, bring forth, engender, from *phunai*, to be born, and finally, from the Indo-European root *bheu*, to be, exist, grow.

There is, in short, no materialist theory of history, deeply grounded in nature and social nature; grounded in the material dialectic, the contradiction between life and the historical conditions of life, which propels the evolution of man in society and, as Marx so often writes, ceaselessly brings the new society to birth from the womb of the old; no theory of history, in short, grounded in the labor metaphysic. As Eric Hobsbaum writes: "The importance of these peculiarities of Marxism," i.e., the so-called labor metaphysic, "is in the field of history, for it is they which allow it to explain—unlike other structural-functional models of society—why and how societies change and transform themselves; in other words, the fact of social evolution. The immense strength of Marx has always lain in his insistence on both the existence of social structure and its historicity, or in other words its internal dynamic of change."[35]

Despite his own vaunted historicism, Mills has no grasp of this revolutionary dynamism, so that he continually looks back. For the same reason, although he would like to enroll himself as a "plain Marxist," his posture remains essentially liberal, moreover, for the most part he makes Marx out to be a liberal, a "radical" liberal, in his own image, upholding the ideals of nineteenth century liberalism. Thus, he fails to transcend bourgeois thought, which is to say, perhaps, as Martin Shaw argues, that he fails to transcend sociology itself, the bourgeois science of society. He remains locked into the inherent conservatism of his discipline and its tradition, locked into Comte's "social statics," with the problematical "social dynamics," from Comte to Parsons, still out of his grasp.[36]

Now the root, once again, is man. Liberalism, indeed, as Mills writes, "has no theory of man in society, no theory of man as the maker of history." Mills would like to have such a theory, such an image; he looks for it in Marx but fails to bring it into focus behind the blinkers of history and biography.

The essence of man, we will remember, is as Marx writes, "the ensemble of social relations." Or as Mills puts it, "The principle of historical specificity includes the nature of human nature." We may agree—but already we are teetering on the edge of the abyss of socialization, rationalization and manipulation. Already we are falling into the Weberian pit of the cheerful robot. For, according to Mills, Marx's "views of human nature are fragmentary, it seems to me, but most of his assumptions about the nature of man are in line with the most adequate assumptions of contemporary social psychology."[37]

Is this the social psychology of Gerth and Mills, the theory of character and social structure, belabored in the dismal fifties, which Mills himself, in a pungent Marxist locution, once dismissed as "a lot of crap"? Is this the social psychology, infecting Mills from the earliest days, as a cornerstone of sociological theory, which conjures man away into a collection of "roles," of internalized "structures of authority," "master symbols," and, once again, "vocabularies of motives"; the social psychology, with language, Mills' early preoccupation, as its pivot, which debases language into a "mechanism of internalization" and hence of "social control"?

A person is composed of an internalization of organized social roles; language is the mechanism by which these internalizations occur. It is the medium in which these roles are organized. Now, we have defined role as a conduct pattern of a person which is typically expected by other persons. It is an expected pattern of conduct. The roles a person plays thus integrate one segment of his total conduct with a segment of the conduct of others. And this integration of persons, and of the roles they expect of one another, occurs by means of language.[38]

We find in Marx two propositions; that there is a human essence and that this essence is sociohistorical. For indeed, the essence of man is not "status conduct"—not emulation, simulation, and dissimulation; not role-playing—but collective labor; productivity; appropriating the world for human enjoyment. It is not the mirror-world of appearances, as in Genet's drama of history, *The Balcony*, but the objective being—the "non-role player," as Zygmunt Bauman, a Polish Marxist sociologist, writes—who smashes this world;[39] it is the objectification of man in nature and nature in man. ("Money," as Marx writes, "is the alienated essence of man"; for it is the *inhuman* power of appropriating the world; the power—and here we should recall Mills' own theories of power—not of living labor, but of cold cash.)

As such the human essence is ever evolving, ever developing; for the first premise of history is the needy individual, who labors with his fellows to satisfy his need, and "once a need is satisfied, . . . new needs arise. The production of new needs is the first historical act."[40] Thus, in "high" culture (but all culture—material, esthetic, intellectual—is a unity, from the lowest levels to the highest), satisfaction in music begets a need for more music, in breadth and depth, and brings ever broader and deeper culture to birth.

Now, as Marx writes in an early critique of Hegel, "This process must have a bearer, a subject."[41] Here "Left Hegelians" part from "Right," and Mills the Marxist radical parts from Mills the Weberian conservative. For the Right Hegelians, and for Weber, this subject is "the thinker," ultimately, as Marx writes, "a pure restless revolving within itself."[42] This is alienated man, in essence religious man—the Weberian ghost of consciousness which haunts Mills to the end: "Man alienated from himself is also the thinker alienated from his *nature*, that is, from his natural and human essence. Hence, his thoughts are fixed, ghostly spirits outside nature and man."[43]

For the Left Hegelians, and for Marx—and for Mills the Marxist—this subject, as somatism specifies, is "an objective sentient being." As such, as we have had occasion to note earlier, he is "therefore a *suffering* being, and since he feels his suffering, he is a *passionate* being. Passion is man's essential capacity energetically bent on its object."[44]

Here in the sphere of passion is Mills, although not without passion, most deeply divided. For what is this passional energy bent on its object but Mills' vaunted craftsmanship? But consider:

The person may become attached to the skill aspects of his roles in such a way that his feelings transcend the orienting function of the institution of which he is a part. Such internalized standards are involved in all "craftsmanship," and groups, such as the guild, may have high ethical and status codes which keep standards of skill high. . . Craftsmanship also refers to the joyful experience of mastering the resistance of the materials with which one works, or the solution of self-imposed tasks—an experience that might occur irrespective of the opinions of other persons or of any rule that exists.[45]

Between the role player, internalizing the opinions of significant others (recall Mills' "opinion" model of democratic political discourse), and the craftsman, energetically bent on his task, irrespective of these opinions, there is an irreparable fracture. This cleavage between the mind and the senses, thought and action, consciousness and being, between the mind metaphysic and the labor metaphysic—this essential religiosity, which Weber affirms and Marx denies, this "German ideology," in Marx's words—is the leading, the fateful, and the conclusive theme of Mills' work.

# Notes and References

*Preface*

1. Richard Gillam "C. Wright Mills: The Intellectual as Rebel" unpublished Master's Essay, Columbia University, 1966 p.16.
2. Robert A. Nisbet, *The Sociological Tradition,* (New York, 1966), p. 251.

*Chapter One*

1. Gillam, *op cit.*, p. 16.
2. *Ibid.*, p. 53.
3. Hans Gerth, *C. Wright Mills, 1916–1962: Studies on the Left*, Vol. 2, No. 3 (1962), 7–11.
4. Robert K. Merton, *Social Theory and Social Structure* (New York, 1967), p. 458.
5. *Sociology and Pragmatism* (New York, 1966), p. 225.
6. "Language, Logic and Culture," in Irving Horowitz, ed., *Power, Politics, and People: The Collected Essays of C. Wright Mills* (New York, n.d.), p. 423.
7. *Ibid.*, p. 424.
8. Emile Durkheim, *Socialism* (New York, 1962).
9. "Language, Logic and Culture," p. 424.
10. Mao Tse-tung, *Four Essays on China and World Communism* (New York, 1972), p. 134.
11. *Ibid.*
12. *Ibid.*, p. 136.
13. "The Language and Ideas of Ancient China," in Horowitz, ed., p. 498.
14. *Ibid.*, p. 478.
15. *Ibid.*, p. 520.
16. *Ibid.*, p. 471.
17. Karl Marx, *Writings of the Young Marx on Philosophy and Society*, ed. and tr. by Loyd D. Easton and Kurt H. Guddat (Garden City, N.Y., 1967), pp. 414–15.
18. "The Language and Ideas of Ancient China," p. 474.
19. Max Weber, *The Protestant Ethic and the Spirit of Capitalism* (New York, 1958), p. 183.

20. *Ibid.*, p. 55.
21. *Ibid.*
22. C. B. MacPherson, *The Political Theory of Possessive Individualism* (London, Oxford, New York, 1972), p. 156.
23. "Language, Logic and Culture," p. 426.
24. *Ibid.*, p. 432.
25. *Ibid.*, p. 433.
26. Emile Durkheim, *Selected Writings*, ed. Anthony Giddens (Cambridge, 1972), pp. 228–29.
27. "Language, Logic and Culture," p. 427.
28. "Reflection, Behavior, and Culture," Master's Essay, University of Texas, Austin, Texas, 1939.
29. Paul Goodman, *Speaking and Language: Defense of Poetry* (New York, 1971), p. 19.
30. Simeon Potter, *Language in the Modern World* (Baltimore, Md., 1960), p. 176.
31. Marx, *Writings of the Young Marx*, p. 421.
32. "Language, Logic and Culture," pp. 433–39.
33. "The Language and Ideas of Ancient China," p. 483.
34. Remy C. Kwant, *Phenomenology of Language* (Pittsburgh, Pa., 1965), p. 122.
35. "Reflection, Behavior, and Culture," p. 60.
36. *Ibid.*, p. 42.
37. Marx, *Writings of the Young Marx*, p. 325.
38. Lionel Trilling, *Freud and the Crisis of Our Culture* (Boston, 1955), p. 48.
39. *Ibid.*, pp. 53–54.
40. Ernest Becker, "Mills' Social Psychology and the Problem of Alienation," in Irving Louis Horowitz, ed., *The New Sociology* (London, Oxford, New York, 1964), p. 110.
41. *Character and Social Structure* (New York, 1964), p. 113.
42. Becker, "Mills' Social Psychology," p. 126. See Durkheim, *The Division of Labor in Society* (New York, 1964).
43. William I. Thomas and Florian Znaniecki, "Three Types of Personality," in C. Wright Mills, ed., *Images of Man* (New York, 1961), p. 421.
44. "Situated Actions and Vocabularies of Motive," in Horowitz, *op. cit.*, p. 442.
45. *Ibid.*, p. 444.
46. *Ibid.*, pp. 447–48.
47. *Ibid.*, p. 450.
48. Weber, "The Protestant Sects and the Spirit of Capitalism," in Hans Gerth and C. Wright Mills, *From Max Weber: Essays in Sociology* (New York, 1949), p. 320.
49. Durkheim, *Suicide* (Glencoe, Ill., 1951), p. 299.
50. Durkheim, *Division of Labor in Society*, p. 129.

## Chapter Two

1. Harvey Swados, *A Radical at Large* (London, 1968), p. 201.
2. Gilam "C. Wright Mills," Master's Essay, p. 70.
3. *Ibid.*, p. 110.
4. *Sociology and Pragmatism*, p. 35.
5. Walter Benjamin, "The Author as Producer," *New Left Review*, No. 62 (July–August, 1970).
6. *Sociology and Pragmatism*, p. 36.
7. *Ibid.*, p. 58.
8. *Ibid.*, p. 60.
9. *Ibid.*, pp. 35–53 *inter alia*.
10. *Ibid.*, p. 53.
11. Quoted by Mills, *ibid.*, p. 154.
12. *Ibid.*, pp. 91–92.
13. *Ibid.*, p. 105.
14. *Ibid.*, p. 110.
15. *Ibid.*, p. 85.
16. *Ibid.*, p. 141.
17. *Ibid.*, p. 124.
18. *Ibid.*, p. 136.
19. Quoted in Manley Thompson, *The Pragmatic Philosophy of C. S. Peirce* (Chicago, 1962), p. 73.
20. *Sociology and Pragmatism*, p. 163.
21. *Ibid.*, p. 150.
22. *Ibid.*, p. 151.
23. *Ibid.*, p. 194.
24. *Ibid.*, p. 152.
25. Marx, *Writings of the Young Marx*, p. 333.
26. *Sociology and Pragmatism*, p. 168.
27. *Ibid.*, p. 188.
28. Quoted by Mills, *ibid.*, p. 171.
29. *Ibid.*, p. 194.
30. *Ibid.*, p. 158.
31. Henry David Aiken, "Review of Mills, *Sociology and Pragmatism*," *New York Review of Books*, IV, 3 (March 11, 1965), 8–10.
32. Jean-Paul Sartre, *Being and Nothingness*, tr. Hazel Barnes (New York, 1956), p. 489.
33. Aiken, "Review of Mills, *Sociology and Pragmatism*."
34. *Sociology and Pragmatism*, p. 221.
35. *Ibid.*, p. 223.
36. *Ibid.*, p. 242.
37. *Ibid.*, p. 249.
38. *Ibid.*, p. 254.
39. *Ibid.*, p. 252.
40. *Ibid.*, p. 255.

41. *Ibid.*, p. 270.
42. *Ibid.*, p. 271.
43. *Ibid.*, p. 273.
44. *Ibid.*, p. 363.
45. *Ibid.*, p. 361.
46. *Ibid.*, p. 363.
47. *Ibid.*, p. 364.
48. *Ibid.*, p. 160.
49. *Ibid.*, p. 405.
50. Dewey, quoted by Mills, *ibid.*, p. 282.
51. Dewey, quoted by Mills, *ibid.*, p. 292.
52. *Ibid.*, p. 426.
53. *Ibid.*, p. 446.
54. *Ibid.*, p. 402.
55. *Ibid.*, p. 423.
56. *Ibid.*, p. 430.
57. *Ibid.*, p. 432.

## Chapter Three

1. "The Nazi Behemoth," review of Franz Neumann, *Behemoth: The Structure and Practice of National Socialism*, in Horowitz, ed., *Power, Politics and People: The Collected Essays of C. Wright Mills*, pp. 177-78.
2. "The Political Gargoyle: Business as Power," in Horowitz, ed., p. 75.
3. *Ibid.*, p. 72.
4. *Ibid.*, p. 74.
5. *Ibid.*, p. 75.
6. *Ibid.*, p. 76.
7. *Ibid.*, pp. 75–76.
8. *Ibid.*
9. *The New Men of Power: America's Labor Leaders* (New York, 1948), p. 290.
10. *Ibid.*, p. 291.
11. "A Marx for the Managers" (with H. H. Gerth), in Horowitz, ed., p. 71.
12. *Ibid.*, p. 63.
13. *Ibid.*, p. 69.
14. *The Marxists* (New York, 1962), p. 117.
15. "A Marx for the Managers," p. 64.
16. Quoted in David Mitrany, *Marx Against the Peasant* (New York, 1961), p. 71.
17. "A Marx for the Managers," p. 60.
18. *The New Men of Power*, p. 6.
19. *Ibid.*, p. 16.
20. *Ibid.*, p. 199.

21. *Ibid.*, pp. 17–19.

22. *Ibid.*, p. 248.

23. *Ibid.*, p. 30.

24. *Ibid.*, p. 31.

25. *Ibid.*, pp. 31–32.

26. *Ibid.*, p. 32.

27. *Ibid.*

28. *Ibid.*, p. 35.

29. *Ibid.*, p. 40.

30. Karl Marx, "The Eighteenth Brumaire of Louis Bonaparte," in Karl Marx and Frederick Engels, *Selected Works* (New York, 1969), p. 97.

31. John Lukacs, *A New History of the Cold War* (Garden City, N.Y., 1966), pp. 344–47.

32. *Ibid.*, pp. 162–63.

33. *The New Men of Power*, pp. 251–52.

34. "Collectivism and the Mixed-up Economy," in Horowitz, ed., p. 180.

35. Gillam, "C. Wright Mills," p. 105.

36. Karl Marx, *The Grundisse*, ed. and tr. by David McLellan (New York, 1971), p. 67.

37. *Ibid.*, p. 68.

38. *The New Men of Power*, pp. 113–14.

39. "Language, Logic and Culture," in Horowitz, ed., p. 427 note.

40. "The Professional Ideology of Social Pathologists," in Horowitz, ed., p. 537.

41. *Ibid.*, p. 536.

42. *White Collar: The American Middle Classes* (New York, 1956), p. 356.

43. *The New Men of Power*, p. 252.

44. Marx, *Writings of the Young Marx*, p. 224.

45. *The New Men of Power*, p. 282.

46. *Ibid.*, p. 253.

47. *Ibid.*

48. Andre Gorz, *Strategy for Labor: A Radical Proposal* (Boston, 1964), p. 51.

49. *The New Men in Power*, p. 254.

50. *Ibid.*, p. 261.

51. *Ibid.*, p. 255.

52. *Ibid.*, p. 257.

53. *Ibid.*, p. 263.

54. *Ibid.*, p. 253.

55. *Ibid.*, p. 291.

56. *Ibid.*, p. 268.

### Chapter Four

1. *White Collar*, p. 323.

2. Herbert Marcuse, *One Dimensional Man* (Boston, 1966), p. xvii.

3. *The New Men of Power*, p. 274.
4. *Ibid.*, p. 281.
5. *White Collar*, pp. 322–23.
6. *Ibid.*, p. xii.
7. *Ibid.*
8. *Ibid.*, p. 4.
9. *Ibid.*, p. 6.
10. *Ibid.*, p. 9.
11. Gillam, p. 53.
12. *White Collar*, p. 12.
13. *Ibid.*, p. 4.
14. *Ibid.*, p. 5.
15. *Ibid.*, p. 9.
16. *Ibid.*, p. 12.
17. *Ibid.*, p. 7.
18. *Ibid.*, p. 6.
19. *Ibid.*, p. 7.
20. *Ibid.*, p. 19.
21. *Ibid.*, p. 21.
22. *Ibid.*, p. 33.
23. *Ibid.*, p. 30.
24. *Ibid.*, pp. 30–31.
25. See Gillam, p. 15.
26. *White Collar*, p. 28.
27. Quoted by Mills, *Sociology and Pragmatism*, p. 273.
28. *White Collar*, p. 9.
29. Abram Kardiner and Edward Preble, *They Studied Man* (Cleveland and New York, 1969), p. 109.
30. Marx, *Grundisse*, p. 69.
31. *White Collar*, p. 34.
32. *Ibid.*, p. 43.
33. *Ibid.*, p. 44.
34. *Ibid.*, p. 53.
35. *Ibid.*
36. *Ibid.*, p. 54.
37. *Ibid.*, p. 57.
38. *Ibid.*
39. *Ibid.*, p. 58.
40. *Ibid.*, p. 55.
41. *Ibid.*, p. 59.
42. *Ibid.*, p. 65.
43. *Ibid.*, p. 71.
44. *Ibid.*, p. 74.
45. *Ibid.*, p. 77.
46. *Ibid.*, p. 100.

47. *Ibid.*, p. 102.
48. *Ibid.*, p. 108.
49. *Ibid.*, p. 110.
50. *Ibid.*, p. 113.
51. *Ibid.*, p. 115.
52. Quoted in Gillam, p. 51.
53. *White Collar*, p. 130.
54. *Ibid.*, p. 131.
55. *Ibid.*, p. 132.
56. *Ibid.*, p. 136.
57. Oglesby in Carl Oglesby, ed., *The New Left Reader* (New York, 1964), pp. 6–7.
58. *White Collar*, p. 142.
59. *Ibid.*, p. 143.
60. *Ibid.*
61. *Ibid.*, p. 148.
62. *Ibid.*, p. 144.
63. *Ibid.*, p. 145.
64. *Ibid.*, p. 146.
65. *Ibid.*, p. 147.
66. *Ibid.*
67. *Ibid.*, p. 149.
68. *Ibid.*, pp. 149-50.
69. *Ibid.*, p. 156.
70. *Ibid.*, p. 157.
71. *Ibid.*, p. 159.
72. *Ibid.*, p. 148.
73. *Ibid.*, p. 149.
74. Walter Benjamin, "The Author as Producer," *New Left Review*, No. 62 (July–August, 1970), 85.
75. *Ibid.*, p. 87.
76. *Ibid.*, p. 88.
77. *Ibid.*, p. 93.
78. *Ibid.*, p. 87.
79. *Ibid.*
80. *Ibid.*, p. 93.
81. *White Collar*, p. 162.
82. Gorz, *Strategy for Labor*, p. ix.
83. *Ibid.*
84. *White Collar*, pp. 220–22.
85. *Ibid.*, p. 215.
86. Quoted in Gorz, *Strategy for Labor*, p. 116, note.
87. *White Collar*, p. 228.
88. *Ibid.*, p. 137.
89. Quoted in Mills, *Images of Man*, p. 143.

90. Marx, *Writings of the Young Marx*, p. 302.
91. *Ibid.*, p. 304.
92. *White Collar*, p. 325.
93. *Ibid.*, p. 326.
94. *Ibid.*
95. Mills and Patricia J. Salter, "The Barricade and the Bedroom," *Politics* (October, 1945), p. 313.
96. Paul Goodman, "Reply," *Politics* (October, 1945), p. 316.
97. Mills and Salter, *Politics* (October, 1945), p. 315.
98. *White Collar*, p. 327.
99. *Ibid.*, p. 329.
100. *Ibid.*
101. *Ibid.*, p. 328.
102. *Ibid.*, pp. 336–37.
103. "Rights of Man," in *Basic Writings of Thomas Paine* (New York, 1942), p. 97.
104. *White Collar*, p. 350.
105. *Ibid.*, p. 354.

## Chapter Five

1. Norman Mailer, *Advertisements for Myself* (New York, 1960), pp. 170–71.
2. *The Power Elite* (New York, 1959), pp. 1–2.
3. Marx, *Writings of the Young Marx*, p. 297.
4. *The Power Elite*, p. 8.
5. Thomas Hobbes, *Leviathan* (New York, 1950), p. 79.
6. *The Power Elite*, p. 9.
7. Marx, "The Eighteenth Brumaire of Louis Bonaparte," in Marx and Engels, *Selected Works*, pp. 171–72.
8. *The Power Elite*, p. 172.
9. Gerth and Mills, *From Max Weber: Essays in Sociology*, p. 82.
10. Niccolo Machiavelli, *The Prince and Selected Discourses* (New York, 1970), p. 98. (I am indebted for this citation to Professor John Fremstad.)
11. Gerth and Mills, *From Max Weber*, p. 78.
12. Jean-Jacques Rousseau, *The First and Second Discourses* (New York, 1964), p. 173.
13. *The Power Elite*, p. 9.
14. *Ibid.*, p. 4.
15. *Ibid.*, p. 5.
16. *Ibid.*, p. 6.
17. *Ibid.*, p. 18.
18. *Ibid.*, p. 20.
19. *Ibid.*, p. 21.
20. *Ibid.*, p. 22.
21. *Ibid.*

22. Neil Sheehan *et al.*, *The Pentagon Papers* (New York, 1971), p. 11.

23. *Ibid.*, p. 41.

24. *Ibid.*, p. 27.

25. Marx, *Writings of the Young Marx*, p. 312.

26. Richard Rovere, "The Interlocking Overlappers," in G. William Domhoff and Hoyt B. Ballard, eds., *C. Wright Mills and the Power Elite*, 1968, p. 184.

27. Karl Marx and Frederick Engels, *The German Ideology* (Moscow, 1964), p. 88.

28. *Ibid.*, p. 95.

29. *The Power Elite*, p. 277.

30. Herbert Aptheker, "Power in America," in Domkoff and Ballard, eds., p. 159.

31. Marx, *Writings of the Young Marx*, p. 312.

32. T. B. Bottomore, *Elites and Society* (Baltimore, 1970), p. 32.

33. Rosa Luxemburg, *The Russian Revolution and Leninism or Marxism* (Ann Arbor, 1961), p. 93.

34. Leon Trotsky, *Trotsky's Diary in Exile, 1935* (Cambridge, Mass., 1958), pp. 100-03.

35. George Simpson, tr., Emile Durkheim, *The Division of Labor in Society* (New York, 1964), p. ix.

36. *The Marxists*, p. 149.

37. Luxemburg, *The Mass Strike* (New York, 1971), p. 27.

38. *Ibid.*, pp. 29–30.

39. *Ibid.*, p. 49.

40. *The Power Elite*, p. 12.

41. *Ibid.*, p. 115.

42. "The American Political Elite: A Collective Portrait," in Horowitz, ed., *Power, Politics and People: The Collected Essays of C. Wright Mills*, p. 121.

43. *Ibid.*, p. 124.

44. *Ibid.*, p. 126.

45. *Ibid.*, p. 131.

46. *The Power Elite*, p. 269.

47. *Ibid.*

48. *Ibid.*, p. 270.

49. *Ibid.*, p. 272.

50. *Ibid.*, p. 273.

51. *Ibid.*, p. 219.

52. *Ibid.*

53. *Ibid.*, p. 215.

54. *Ibid.*, p. 297.

55. *Ibid.*, p. 309.

56. *Ibid.*, p. 298.

57. *Ibid.*, p. 213.

58. *Ibid.*, pp. 304–05.
59. *Ibid.*, pp. 320–21.
60. *Ibid.*, p. 323.
61. *Ibid.*, pp. 299–230.
62. Karl Mannheim, *Ideology and Utopia* (New York, 1936), p. 150.
63. *The Power Elite*, p. 300.
64. Jerome Ch'en, ed., *Mao Papers* (London, 1970), p. 37.
65. *Ibid.*, p. 39.
66. *Ibid.*, p. 66.
67. *The Power Elite*, p. 307.
68. *Ibid.*, p. 302.
69. Ch'en, *Mao Papers*, p. 123.
70. *The Power Elite*, p. 164.
71. *Ibid.*, p. 162.
72. *Ibid.*, p. 163.
73. Marx and Engels, *The German Ideology*, p. 74.
74. *The Power Elite*, p. 164.
75. *Ibid.*

### Chapter Six

1. *The Causes of World War Three* (New York, 1958), p. 155.
2. *The Sociological Imagination* (New York, 1959), *inter alia*.
3. Mills, *Listen Yankee! The Revolution in Cuba* (New York, 1960), p. 18.
4. *Ibid.*, p. 114.
5. *Ibid.*
6. *Ibid.*, p. 97.
7. *The Sociological Imagination*, p. 5.
8. "Letter to the New Left," included in part in Carl Oglesby, ed., *The New Left Reader*, pp. 27–28.
9. Marx, *Writings of the Young Marx*, p. 259.
10. "Letter to the New Left," p. 31.
11. *The Sociological Imagination*, p. 10.
12. *Ibid.*, p. 5.
13. *Ibid.*, p. 11.
14. *Ibid.*, p. 18.
15. Alvin W. Gouldner, *The Coming Crisis of Western Sociology* (New York, 1971), p. 452.
16. *Ibid.*, p. 352.
17. *The Sociological Imagination*, p. 48.
18. *Ibid.*, p. 82.
19. Gouldner, *The Coming Crisis of Western Sociology*, p. 447.
20. Lukacs, *A New History of the Cold War*, p. 13.
21. *The Sociological Imagination*, p. 26.
22. *Ibid.*, p. 32.
23. *Ibid.*, p. 48, note.

24. *Ibid.*, p. 32.
25. Arnold M. Rose and Caroline B. Rose, *Sociology: The Study of Human Relations* (New York, 1969), p. 144.
26. *Ibid.*
27. Irving Louis Horowitz, *Professing Sociology* (Chicago, 1968), p. 14.
28. Marx, *Writings of the Young Marx*, p. 423.
29. *Ibid.*, p. 437.
30. *Ibid.*, p. 459.
31. *Ibid.*, p. 463.
32. *The Sociological Imagination*, p. 172.
33. Alfred North Whitehead, *Process and Reality* (New York, 1929), p. 38.
34. *The Sociological Imagination*, p. 93.
35. *Listen Yankee!*, p. 165.
36. *Ibid.*, p. 160.
37. Marx, *Writings of the Young Marx*, p. 252.
38. Gouldner, *The Coming Crisis of Western Sociology*, p. 143.
39. *Ibid.*, p. 146.
40. *The Sociological Imagination*, pp. 42–43.
41. *Ibid.*, p. 66.
42. *Ibid.*, p. 120.
43. *Ibid.*
44. Marx, *Writings of the Young Marx*, p. 306.
45. *The Sociological Imagination*, p. 67.
46. *Ibid.*
47. *Ibid.*, pp. 67–68.
48. *Ibid.*, p. 69.
49. *Ibid.*, p. 190.
50. *Ibid.*, p. 101.
51. *Ibid.*, p. 103.
52. Andre Breton, *Manifestos of Surrealism* (Ann Arbor, 1972), p. 129.
53. *The Sociological Imagination*, p. 106.
54. *Ibid.*, p. 103.
55. Paul Goodman, *Compulsory Mis-education and the Community of Scholars* (New York, 1964), p. 292.
56. *The Sociological Imagination*, p. 79.
57. *Ibid.*, pp. 129–30.
58. *Ibid.*, p. 75.
59. *Ibid.*, p. 165.
60. *Ibid.*, p. 167.
61. Gerth and Mills, *From Max Weber*, p. 50.
62. Weber, in Gerth and Mills, *From Max Weber*, p. 169.
63. Gerth and Mills, p. 51.
64. *Ibid.*, p. 50.
65. Weber, Gerth and Mills, p. 85.
66. *The Sociological Imagination*, p. 115.

67. Herbert Marcuse, *Negations* (Boston, 1968), p. 217.

68. *Ibid.*, p. 221.

69. Talcott Parsons, "Max Weber's Sociological Analysis of Capitalism and Modern Institutions," in Harry Elmer Barnes, ed., *An Introduction to the History of Sociology* (Chicago, 1948), p. 301.

70. Marcuse, *Negations*, p. 224.

71. *The Sociological Imagination*, p. 171.

72. *Ibid.*

73. *Ibid.*, p. 169.

74. *Ibid.*, p. 3.

75. *Ibid.*, p. 172.

76. *Ibid.*, p. 171.

77. Marx, *Writings of the Young Marx*, p. 250.

## Chapter Seven

1. *Images of Man: The Classic Tradition in Sociological Thinking* (New York, 1961), p. 3.

2. *Ibid.*, p. 7.

3. Marx, *Writings of the Young Marx*, p. 402.

4. *Ibid.*, p. 314.

5. Nisbet, *The Sociological Tradition*, p. 286.

6. Gerth and Mills, *From Max Weber*, p. 194.

7. *Images of Man*, p. 25.

8. *The Marxists*, p. 12.

9. *Ibid.*, p. 31.

10. *Ibid.*, p. 33.

11. *Ibid.*, pp. 32–33.

12. *Ibid.*, p. 32.

13. *Ibid.*, p. 28.

14. *Ibid.*, p. 33.

15. *Ibid.*, p. 29.

16. *Ibid.*, p. 129.

17. Lenin, quoted in *The Marxists*, p. 215.

18. *The Marxists*, p. 113.

19. *Ibid.*, p. 114.

20. Marx, quoted in *The Marxists*, p. 25.

21. Marx, *Writings of the Young Marx*, p. 250.

22. *Ibid.*, p. 409.

23. *Ibid.*, p. 419.

24. *Ibid.*, p. 258.

25. *Ibid.*, p. 322.

26. *Ibid.*, p. 423.

27. *Ibid.*

28. T. B. Bottomore, *Classes in Modern Society* (New York, 1966), pp. 86-87.

29. Marx, *Writings of the Young Marx*, p. 431.

30. *Ibid*.

31. *The Marxists*, p. 11.

32. *Ibid*., p. 77.

33. Marx, *Writings of the Young Marx*, p. 426.

34. *The Marxists*, p. 81.

35. Eric Hobsbaum, "Karl Marx's Contribution to Historiography," in Robin Blackburn, ed., *Ideology in Social Science* (New York, 1972), p. 274.

36. See Martin Shaw, "The Coming Crisis of Radical Sociology," in Robin Blackburn, ed., pp. 32–44.

37. *The Marxists*, pp. 38–30.

38. Gerth and Mills, *Character and Social Structure* (New York, 1964), p. 83.

39. Zygmunt Bauman, "Modern Times, Modern Marxism," in Peter Berger, ed., *Marxism and Sociology* (New York, 1969), pp. 1–17.

40. Marx, *Writings of the Young Marx*, p. 420.

41. *Ibid*., p. 322.

42. *Ibid*., p. 333.

43. *Ibid*., p. 334.

44. *Ibid*., p. 326.

45. Gerth and Mills, *Character and Social Structure*, pp. 398–99.

# Selected Bibliography

Mills was a prolific writer. Most of his principal writings are discussed in the present volume, and most of them are available in paperback. A complete bibliography may be found in Irving Louis Horowitz, ed., *Power, Politics, and People: The Collected Essays of C. Wright Mills* (New York: Ballantine Books, n.d.). Here are cited books and pamphlets, introductions and anthologies, commentaries, major lectures and addresses, monographs and essays on Mills, and reviews of Mills' work: a total by Mills of 205 items.

Since the publication of *Power, Politics, and People*, Horowitz has published an article on "The Unpublished Writings of C. Wright Mills," in *Studies on the Left*, 3, No. 4, 3-23. A biography of Mills by historian Richard Gillam, whose Master's Essay on Mills is cited in the present volume, is in preparation.

### PRIMARY SOURCES

1. Bibliography

An exhaustive bibliography may be found in Irving Louis Horowitz, ed., *Power, Politics, and People: The Collected Essays of C. Wright Mills* (New York: Ballantine Books, n.d.).

2. Books

*A Sociological Account of Pragmatism.* Ph.d dissertation, University of Wisconsin, 1942. Published in 1966 as *Sociology and Pragmatism* (see below).

*The New Men of Power: America's Labor Leaders.* With the assistance of Helen Schneider. New York: Harcourt, Brace & Company, 1948.

*The Puerto Rican Journey: New York's Newest Migrants.* With Clarence Senior and Rose K. Goldsen. New York: Oxford University Press, 1950.

*White Collar: The American Middle Classes.* New York: Oxford University Press, 1951. This book was Mills' first "popular" success and established him as a leading dissenting social critic.

*Character And Social Structure: The Psychology of Social Institutions.* With Hans H. Gerth. New York: Harcourt, Brace & Company, 1953. This is a labored work in the 1950's mood of apathy and conformity, a true ideological reflection of the period. Mills later dismissed it as "a lot of crap!"

*The Power Elite.* New York: Oxford University Press, 1956. Widely discussed in newspaper columns and on radio and television, it is, as the present volume argues, the hypertrophied expression of the least fruitful of Millsian *aperçus* and styles of social thought and research, although it has spawned a numerous progeny.

*The Causes of World War Three.* New York: Simon & Schuster, 1958. A publisher assured Mills that he could put it in "every drug store in the country".

*The Sociological Imagination.* New York: Oxford University Press, 1959. A genuine wisdom book, as Mills draws near the end of his life.

*Listen, Yankee: The Revolution in Cuba.* New York: McGraw-Hill, An epochal book.

*The Marxists.* New York: Dell, 1963. Mills' last book.

*Power, Politics, and People: The Collected Essays of C. Wright Mills.* Edited by Irving Louis Horowitz. New York: Oxford University Press, 1963. A posthumous collection of Mills' more important short works.

*Sociology And Pragmatism.* New York, Oxford University Press, 1966. Published posthumously. A major work on pragmatism, despite its rough and ready shape.

3. Articles

"Language, Logic, and Culture." *American Sociological Review* 4, no. 5 (October, 1939), 670–80. Included in Horowitz, *Power, Politics, and People.*

"Situated Actions and Vocabularies of Motive." *American Sociological Review* 5, no. 6 (December, 1940), 904–13. Included in Horowitz, *Power, Politics, and People.*

"The Language and Ideas of Ancient China: Marcel Granet's Contribution to the Sociology of Knowledge." In Horowitz, ed., *Power, Politics, and People.* This essay was originally written for a graduate seminar in the University of Wisconsin in 1940.

"The Powerless People: The Role of the Intellectual in Society." *Politics* 1, no. 3 (April, 1944).

"The People In the Unions." With Thelma Ehrlich. *Labor and Nation* 3 (March–April, 1947), 25–29.

"The Political Complexion of Labor Leadership." With Helen Schneider. *Labor and Nation* 3 (July–August, 1947), 9–10.

"White Collar Unionism: Labor and Democracy." *Labor and Nation* 5 (May–June, 1949), 17–21.

"Plain Talk On Fancy Sex: A Peek at Public Morality." *New York Journal American—International News Service Syndicate,* August 31, 1952.

"A Diagnosis of Our Moral Uneasiness." *New York Times Magazine,* November, 1952, pp. 10, 57–59. Included in Horowitz, *Power, Politics, and People.*

"The Complacent Young Men: Reason For Anger." *Anvil and Student Partisan* 9, no. 1 (1958), 13–15.

"Culture And Politics: The Fourth Epoch." *The Listener* 61, no. 1563 (March 12, 1959).

"The Decline of the Left." *Contact*, no. 3 (1959), 5–18.

"Letter To The New Left." *New Left Review*, no. 5 (September–October, 1960), 18–23. A famous document of the era.

"On the New Left." *Studies On the Left* 2, no. 1 (1961), 63–72.

"Modest Proposals for Patriotic Americans." With Saul Landau. *The Tribune* (London), May 19, 1961.

"Intellectuals and Russia." *Dissent* 6, no. 3 (Summer, 1959), 295–98.

SECONDARY SOURCES

1. Books and articles on Mills

APTHEKER, HERBERT. *The World of C. Wright Mills*. New York: Marzani and Munsell, 1960. A critique of Mills from the point of view of a rather narrow doctrinaire Marxism. Some good correctional points are made.

BOULKE, ROBERT H., and WINETROUT, KENNETH. *Bureaucrats and Intellectuals: A Critique of C. Wright Mills*. Springfield, Mass.: American International College, 1963.

BOTTOMORE, TOM B. "American Heretics." *Archive of European Sociology* 1 (1960), 289–96. An early approach to the "mythos" of Mills.

CLECAK, PETER. *Radical Paradoxes: Dilemmas of the American Left, 1945–1970*. New York: Harper & Row, 1973. This recent book treats Mills, along with the economist Paul Sweezy and the philosopher Herbert Marcuse, as a major "radical critic" in the postwar years, and a pivotal figure in the Left movement of the 1960s. It yields important perspectives on its subject-matter.

DOMHOFF, G. WILLIAM, and BALLARD, HOYT B., eds. *C. Wright Mills and The Power Elite*. Boston, Beacon Press, 1968. An important collection of articles by liberals, Marxists, and Millsians, focusing on the contraversial theme of "the power elite."

GERTH, HANS H. "C. Wright Mills, 1916–1962." *Studies On the Left* 2, no. 3 (1963), 7–15. A memorial piece by Mills' long-time teacher, friend, and collaborator.

GILLAM, RICHARD. "The Intellectual As Rebel: C. Wright Mills, 1916–1946." M.A. thesis, Columbia University, 1969. This important work is expected to appear soon as *C. Wright Mills: The Lone Rebel*.

HOROWITZ, IRVING A. "The Unfinished Writings of C. Wright Mills." *Studies On the Left* 3, no. 4 (1964), 3–23.

————. *C. Wright Mills' White Collar: A Critical Commentary*. New York: American R. D. M. Corp., 1967. By a leading "left" sociologist who has done much to publicize Mills' thought.

————, ed. *The New Sociology: Essays in Honor of C. Wright Mills*. New York: Oxford University Press, 1964. A valuable collection of articles, psychological and philosophical, as well as sociological, by a panoply of scholars.

MILIBAND, RALPH A. "C. Wright Mills," *New Left Review,* no. 5 (May-June, 1962), 5–20. By a leading admirer of Mills in England.

PERLMAN, FREDY. *The Incoherence of the Intellectual: C. Wright Mills' Struggle to Unite Knowledge and Action.* Detroit: Black & Red, 1970. A remarkable practico-theoretical critique of Mills, from a Marxist-anarchist point of view.

SWADOS, HARVEY. *A Radical's America.* Boston: Little, Brown, 1962. Contains a fascinating personal memoir of Mills, dating from the early 1940s.

SWEEZY, PAUL M. "Power Elite Or Ruling Class." *Monthly Review,* September, 1956, pp. 138–39.

2. Books influenced by Mills

DOMHOFF, G. WILLIAM. *The Bohemian Grove and Other Retreats: A Study in Ruling Class Cohesiveness.* New York: Harper & Row, 1975.

———. *Higher Circles: The Governing Circles in America.* New York: Random House, 1971.

———. *Who Rules America.* New York: Prentice Hall, 1967.

GORZ, ANDRE. *Strategy For Labor: A Radical Proposal.* Boston: Beacon Press, 1964. This germinal work appears to have an unacknowledged debt to Mills' strategy for labor democracy.

MARCUSE, HERBERT. *One Dimensional Man.* Boston: Beacon Press, 1966. This eminent philosopher, the so-called philosopher of the New Left, acknowledges an important debt to Mills.

MILIBAND, RALPH. *State in Capitalist Society: An Analysis of the Western System of Power.* New York: Basic Books, 1969.

# Index